The Enchanted Isles

The Enchanted Isles

Herman Melville

ET REMOTISSIMA PROPE

100 PAGES

100 PAGES

Published by Hesperus Press Limited
4 Rickett Street, London sw6 1ru
www.hesperuspress.com

First published as *The Encantadas or Enchanted Isles* in 1854
First published by Hesperus Press Limited, 2002

Foreword © Margaret Drabble, 2002

Designed and typeset by Fraser Muggeridge
Printed in the United Arab Emirates by Oriental Press

isbn: 1-84391-015-2

CONTENTS

FOREWORD

Herman Melville sailed on the *Acushnet* to the Enchanted Isles in 1841 as a young man. It was his first whaling voyage. It is unlikely that he ever saw these islands again, but he revisited them many times in his imagination, transforming them into something rich and strange, as he transformed the *Acushnet* into the mythical *Pequod*. The ten sketches were written in the doldrums that followed the publication of his masterpiece, *Moby-Dick*, in 1851, when Melville's literary career seemed to have lost its course. He was still young, but he was beset by financial troubles. He was living inland in rural Massachusetts, struggling to keep his growing family, as a farmer and freelance author. Things were not going well for him professionally, and the stories were first published pseudonymously, in *Putnam's*, in 1854, as *The Encantadas or Enchanted Isles*, by 'Salvator R. Tarnmoor', rather than proudly, under his own name. Because of this, and because of comments by his wife on 'the strain on his health in the spring of 1853', and because of the fragmented nature of the narrative, it became customary to detect in them a sign of a waning of his creative powers. But it is now widely recognised that we have here some of the most stirring and evocative prose that Melville ever wrote.

The Enchanted Isles – so called for their unchartered and apparently wandering behaviour – are better known today as the Galapagos, which Charles Darwin had visited six years earlier than Melville. They have become famous as the inspiration for Darwin's theory of evolution, and we now think of them as a zoologist's paradise. But to Melville they seemed to present a much bleaker aspect. As he pictures forth these bleak, barren volcanic islands, he dwells again and again on their inhospitable terrain, their reptilian inhabitants, their blackened and demonic landscapes, and the cruelties that they bred amongst the men who were cast upon their shores. He paints an infernal domination that belongs more to Caliban than to Prospero, and his vision draws more from Milton's Hell than from his Heaven. These islands are, literally, the graveyard of hope and of love. They are a mis-creation, an unnatural abortion. Melville even describes the innocent penguin as an abased and ungainly failure of creation, 'the most ambiguous and least lovely creature yet discovered by man' – a portrait which few today would recognise.

And yet, and yet… As Milton wrote with passion of his Pandemonium, and Dante of his Inferno, so Melville seems more than half in love with his own monstrous invention. How else could he write with such energy of those arrested torrents of tormented lava, of 'the ballroom blaze' of the burning volcano, and of the Plutonian sight of those 'dark vitrified masses'? The landscape rises before us as we read, and breaks upon us with extraordinary vitality, surging upon us as the lava long ago surged up from the ocean bed. These scenes may not be conventionally beautiful, but they are sublime. They are a supreme representation of Edmund Burke's influential concept of the sublime, as outlined in his philosophical enquiry into the origin of '…*our ideas of the Sublime and the Beautiful*' (1757). We find here many classic invocations of the sublime, drawn from the dark vistas of the industrial revolution, with its clinkers, smithies and chimney-stacks, and from the architectural grandeur of battlements and palaces and cathedrals and – most classic of all – the

Roman Coliseum. Melville compares, he alludes, he quotes, as he attempts, with a dazzling poetic richness of vocabulary, to give these strange and novel phenomena a literary ancestry. He enlists Spenser and Chatterton and William Collins in his (occasionally adapted) epigraphs, leaving us no doubt that he is writing something more fantastic, less subdued to fact, than a travelogue. Yet the overall impression breaks free from this literary web of references, and leaves the reader with a sense of overwhelming and original strangeness. These islands are beyond comparisons: they and their natural inhabitants are like nothing we have ever seen before. Melville shows us a world before the birth of man. 'Here hues were seen as yet unpainted, and figures which are unengraved.'

Paradoxically, despite Melville's insistence on bleakness and melancholy, he manages to convey a deeper sense of stubborn exhilaration. His descriptions of the giant tortoises, surely among the finest passages he ever wrote, are charged with a remarkable mixture of emotions. These creatures, the original native lords of the island, are, he tells us, expressive of 'lasting sorrow and penal hopelessness', and the memory of them has haunted him at home in the picturesque scenery of his native Adirondack Mountains. His account of his first night vision of the three 'huge antediluvian-looking tortoises', and of the sound of their dragging themselves about on the deck above him, has a strange drugged dream-like quality that recalls the reveries of Thomas De Quincey. The tortoises are the island: the battle scars are its history, and they represent the long history of creation. They are hopeless, obstinate, infatuated, but they will not give up. They are possessed of infinite endurance, and part of Melville is moved to a profound respect for their heroic and pointless persistence. Like Melville's great fictional creation, Bartleby, they will not be deflected from their course. The spirit is stubborn, and it endures.

The fleeting human jetsam of the islands possesses less majesty than the tortoises, yet some of the basest of humans have a curious dignity, and they are not untouched by the spirit of the place. Even the buccaneers, Melville supposes, were infused at times by 'pure peacefulness and kindly fellowship with nature'. He writes of lawless 'cowboys of the sea', of the ferocious rabble of the Dog-King, and of other desperadoes, but he writes of them with a certain sympathy, and with respect. These are not the subhuman savages that his great maritime successor Conrad would later evoke. The account of Oberlus, the potato grower of Hood's Isle – a portrait based on various accounts of the life of an Irishman, Patrick Watkins – appears to condemn his surly and brutal behaviour, yet at the same time exalts him as a force of nature: 'He struck strangers much as if he were a volcanic creature thrown up by the same convulsion which exploded into sight the isle.' We cannot doubt that something in Melville himself responded to the lonely and stubborn misanthropy of his characters, as it did to the peculiar grandeur, at once natural and unnatural, of the islands he visited so briefly at the age of twenty-one – the age at which, he tells us, the poor lieutenant of the US frigate *Essex*, buried on James's Isle, attained his majority in death.

– *Margaret Drabble, 2002*

The Enchanted Isles

Sketch First
The Isles at Large

That may not be, said then the ferryman,
Least we unweeting hap to be fordonne;
For those same islands seeming now and than,
Are not firme land, nor any certein wonne,
But stragling plots which to and fro do ronne
In the wide waters; therefore are they hight
The Wandering Islands; therefore do them shonne;
For they have oft drawne many a wandring wight
Into most deadly daunger and distressed plight;
For whosoever once hath fastened
His foot thereon may never it secure
But wandreth evermore uncertein and unsure.

Darke, dolefull, dreary, like a greedy grave,
That still for carrion carcasses doth crave;
On top whereof ay dwelt the ghastly owl,
Shrieking his balefull note, which ever drave
Far from that haunt all other cheerful fowl,
And all about it wandring ghosts did wayle and howl.

Take five and twenty heaps of cinders dumped here and there in an outside city lot, imagine some of them magnified into mountains, and the vacant lot the sea, and you will have a fit idea of the general aspect of the Encantadas, or Enchanted Isles. A group rather of extinct volcanoes than of isles, looking much as the world at large might after a penal conflagration.

It is to be doubted whether any spot on earth can, in desolateness, furnish a parallel to this group. Abandoned cemeteries of long ago, old cities by piecemeal tumbling to their ruin, these are melancholy enough; but, like all else which has but once been associated with humanity, they still awaken in us some thoughts of sympathy, however sad. Hence, even the Dead Sea, along with whatever other emotions it may at times inspire, does not fail to touch in the pilgrim some of his less unpleasurable feelings.

And as for solitariness, the great forests of the north, the expanses of unnavigated waters, the Greenland ice-fields, are the profoundest of solitudes to a human observer; still the magic of their changeable tides and seasons mitigates their terror, because, though unvisited by men, those forests are visited by the May, the remotest seas reflect familiar stars even as Lake Erie does, and in the clear air of a fine polar day, the irradiated, azure ice shows beautifully as malachite.

But the special curse, as one may call it, of the Encantadas, that which exalts them in desolation above Idumea[1] and the Pole, is that to them change never comes – neither the change of seasons nor of sorrows. Cut by the equator, they know not autumn, and they know not spring; while, already reduced to the lees of fire, ruin itself can work little more upon them. The showers refresh the deserts, but in these isles rain never falls. Like split Syrian gourds left withering in the sun, they are cracked by an everlasting drought beneath a torrid sky. 'Have mercy upon me,' the wailing spirit of the Encantadas seems to cry, 'and send Lazarus that he may dip the tip of his finger in water and cool my tongue, for I am tormented in this flame.'

Another feature in these isles is their emphatic uninhabitableness. It is deemed a fit type of all-forsaken overthrow that the jackal should den in the wastes of weedy Babylon, but the Encantadas refuse to harbour even the outcasts of the beasts. Man and wolf alike disown them. Little but reptile life is here found: tortoises, lizards, immense spiders, snakes, and that strangest anomaly of outlandish nature, the iguana. No voice, no low, no howl is heard – the chief sound of life here is a hiss.

On most of the isles where vegetation is found at all, it is more ungrateful than the blankness of Aracama. Tangled thickets of wiry bushes, without fruit and without a name, springing up among deep fissures of calcined rock and treacherously masking them, or a parched growth of distorted cactus trees.

In many places the coast is rock-bound, or, more properly, clinker-bound; tumbled masses of blackish or greenish stuff like the dross of an iron furnace, forming dark clefts and caves here and there, into which a ceaseless sea pours a fury of foam, overhanging them with a swirl of grey, haggard mist, amidst which sail screaming flights of unearthly birds heightening the dismal din. However calm the sea without, there is no rest for these swells and those rocks; they lash and are lashed, even when the outer ocean is most at peace with itself. On the oppressive, clouded days, such as are peculiar to this part of the watery equator, the dark vitrified masses, many of which raise themselves among white whirlpools and breakers in detached and perilous places off the shore, present a most Plutonian sight. In no world but a fallen one could such lands exist.

Those parts of the strand free from the marks of fire stretch away in wide level beaches of multitudinous dead shells, with here and there decayed bits of sugar cane, bamboo, and coconuts, washed upon this other and darker world from the charming palm isles to the westward and southward, all the way from Paradise to Tartarus, while mixed with the relics of distant beauty you will sometimes see fragments of charred wood and mouldering ribs of wrecks. Neither will anyone be surprised at meeting these last, after observing the conflicting currents which eddy throughout nearly all the wide channels of the entire group. The capriciousness of the tides of air sympathises with those of the sea. Nowhere is the wind so light, baffling, and every way unreliable, and so given to perplexing calms as at the Encantadas. Nigh a month has been spent by a ship going from one isle to another, though but ninety miles between; for owing to the force of the current, the boats employed to tow barely suffice to keep the craft from sweeping upon the cliffs, but do nothing towards accelerating her voyage. Sometimes it is impossible for a vessel from afar to fetch up with the group itself, unless large allowances for prospective leeway have been made ere its coming in sight. And yet, at other times, there is a mysterious indraught, which irresistibly draws a passing vessel among the isles, though not bound to them.

True, at one period, as to some extent at the present day, large fleets of whalemen cruised for spermaceti upon what some seamen call the Enchanted Ground. But this, as in due place will be described, was off the great outer isle of Albemarle[2], away from the intricacies of the smaller isles, where there is plenty of sea room, and hence to that vicinity the above remarks do not altogether apply, though even there the current runs at times with singular force, shifting, too, with as singular a caprice.

Indeed, there are seasons when currents quite unaccountable prevail for a great distance round about the total group, and are so strong and irregular as to change a vessel's course against the helm, though sailing at the rate of four or five miles the hour. The difference in the reckonings of navigators produced by these causes, along with the light and variable winds, long nourished a persuasion that there existed two distinct clusters of isles in the parallel of the Encantadas, about a hundred leagues apart. Such was the idea of their earlier visitors, the buccaneers; and as late as 1750 the charts of that part of the Pacific accorded with the strange delusion. And this apparent fleetingness and unreality of the locality of the isles was most probably one reason for the Spaniards calling them the Encantada, or Enchanted Group.

But not uninfluenced by their character, as they now confessedly exist, the modern voyager will be inclined to fancy that the bestowal of this name might have in part originated in that air of spellbound desertness which so significantly invests the isles. Nothing can better suggest the aspect of once living things malignly crumbled from ruddiness into ashes. Apples of Sodom, after touching, seem these isles.

However wavering their place may seem by reason of the currents, they themselves, at least to one upon the shore, appear invariably the same: fixed, cast, glued into the very body of cadaverous death.

Nor would the appellation 'enchanted' seem misapplied in still another sense. For concerning the peculiar reptile inhabitant of these wilds – whose presence gives the group its second Spanish name, Galapagos – concerning the tortoises found here, most mariners have long cherished a superstition not more frightful than grotesque. They earnestly believe that all wicked sea officers, more especially commodores and captains, are at death (and in some cases before death) transformed into tortoises, thenceforth dwelling upon these hot aridities, sole solitary lords of asphaltum.

Doubtless, so quaintly dolorous a thought was originally inspired by the woebegone landscape itself, but more particularly, perhaps, by the tortoises. For, apart from their strictly physical features, there is something strangely self-condemned in the appearance of these creatures. Lasting sorrow and penal hopelessness are in no animal form so suppliantly expressed as in theirs; while the thought of their wonderful longevity does not fail to enhance the impression.

Nor even at the risk of meriting the charge of absurdly believing in enchantments can I restrain the admission that sometimes, even now, when leaving the crowded city to wander out July and August among the Adirondack Mountains, far from the influences of towns, and proportionally nigh to the mysterious ones of nature; when at such times I sit me down in the mossy head of some deep-wooded gorge, surrounded by prostrate trunks of blasted pines, and recall, as in a dream, my other and far-distant rovings in the baked heart of the charmed isles, and remember the sudden glimpses of dusky shells, and long languid necks protruded from the leafless thickets, and again have beheld the vitreous inland rocks worn down and grooved into deep ruts by ages and ages of the slow draggings of tortoises in quest of pools of scanty water, I can hardly resist the feeling that in my time I have indeed slept upon evilly enchanted ground.

Nay, such is the vividness of my memory, or the magic of my fancy, that I know not whether I am not the occasional victim of optical delusion concerning the Galapagos. For, often in scenes of social merriment, and especially at revels held by candlelight in old-fashioned mansions – so that shadows are thrown into the further recesses of an angular and spacious room, making them put on a look of haunted undergrowth of lonely woods – I have drawn the attention of my comrades by my fixed gaze and sudden change of air, as I have seemed to see, slowly emerging from those imagined solitudes, and heavily crawling along the floor, the ghost of a gigantic tortoise, with 'Memento * * * * *' burning in live letters upon his back.

Sketch Second
Two Sides to a Tortoise

Most ugly shapes and horrible aspects,
Such as Dame Nature selfe mote feare to see,
Or shame, that ever should so fowle defects
From her most cunning hand escaped bee;
All dreadfull pourtraicts of deformitee.
Ne wonder if these do a man appall;
For all that here at home we dreadfull hold
Be but as bugs to fearen babes withall
Compared to the creatures in these isles' entrall.

Fear naught, then said the palmer, well avized,
For these same monsters are not there indeed,
But are into these fearful shapes disguized.

And lifting up his vertuous staffe on high,
Then all that dreadful armie fast gan flye
Into great Zethy's bosom, where they hidden lye.

In view of the description given, may one be gay upon the Encantadas? Yes: that is, find one the gaiety, and he will be gay. And, indeed, sackcloth and ashes as they are, the isles are not perhaps unmitigated gloom. For while no spectator can deny their claims to a most solemn and superstitious consideration, (no more than my firmest resolutions can decline to behold the spectre-tortoise when emerging from its shadowy recess), yet even the tortoise, dark and melancholy as it is upon the back, still possesses a bright side; its calipee or breastplate being sometimes of a faint yellowish or golden tinge. Moreover, everyone knows that tortoises, as well as turtles, are of such a make that if you but put them on their backs you thereby expose their bright sides without the possibility of their recovering themselves, and turning into view the other. But after you have done this, and because you have done this, you should not swear that the tortoise has no dark side. Enjoy the bright, keep it turned up perpetually if you can, but be honest, and don't deny the black. Neither should he who cannot turn the tortoise from its natural position so as to hide the darker and expose his livelier aspect, like a great October pumpkin in the sun, for that cause declare the creature to be one total inky blot. The tortoise is both black and bright. But let us to particulars.

Some months before my first stepping ashore upon the group, my ship was cruising in its close vicinity. One noon we found ourselves off the south head of Albemarle, and not very far from the land. Partly by way of freak, and partly by way of spying out so strange a country, a boat's crew was sent ashore, with orders to see all they could, and, besides, bring back whatever tortoises they could conveniently transport.

It was after sunset when the adventurers returned. I

looked down over the ship's high side as if looking down over the curb of a well, and dimly saw the damp boat deep in the sea with some unwonted weight. Ropes were dropped over, and presently three huge antediluvian-looking tortoises, after much straining, were landed on deck. They seemed hardly of the seed of earth. We had been broad upon the waters for five long months, a period amply sufficient to make all things of the land wear a fabulous hue to the dreamy mind. Had three Spanish custom-house officers boarded us then it is not unlikely that I should have curiously stared at them, felt of them, and stroked them, much as savages serve civilised guests. But instead of three custom-house officers, behold these really wondrous tortoises – none of your schoolboy mud-turtles, but black as widower's weeds, heavy as chests of plate, with vast shells medallioned and orbed like shields, and dented and blistered like shields that have breasted a battle, shaggy, too, here and there, with dark green moss, and slimy with the spray of the sea. These mystic creatures, suddenly translated by night from unutterable solitudes to our peopled deck, affected me in a manner not easy to unfold. They seemed newly crawled forth from beneath the foundations of the world. Yea, they seemed the identical tortoises whereon the Hindu plants this total sphere. With a lantern I inspected them more closely. Such worshipful venerableness of aspect! Such furry greenness mantling the rude peelings and healing the fissures of their shattered shells. I no more saw three tortoises. They expanded – became transfigured. I seemed to see three Roman coliseums in magnificent decay.

'Ye oldest inhabitants of this or any other isle,' said I,

'pray, give me the freedom of your three-walled towns.'

The great feeling inspired by these creatures was that of age: dateless, indefinite endurance. And, in fact, that any other creature can live and breathe as long as the tortoise of the Encantadas, I will not readily believe. Not to hint of their known capacity of sustaining life while going without food for an entire year, consider that impregnable armour of their living mail. What other bodily being possesses such a citadel wherein to resist the assaults of Time?

As, lantern in hand, I scraped among the moss and beheld the ancient scars of bruises received in many a sullen fall among the marly mountains of the isle – scars strangely widened, swollen, half obliterate, and yet distorted like those sometimes found in the bark of very hoary trees; I seemed an antiquary of a geologist, studying the bird tracks and ciphers upon the exhumed slates trod by incredible creatures whose very ghosts are now defunct.

As I lay in my hammock that night, overhead I heard the slow weary draggings of the three ponderous strangers along the encumbered deck. Their stupidity or their resolution was so great that they never went aside for any impediment. One ceased his movements altogether just before the mid-watch. At sunrise I found him butted like a battering ram against the immovable foot of the foremast, and still striving, tooth and nail, to force the impossible passage. That these tortoises are the victims of a penal, or malignant, or perhaps a downright diabolical enchanter, seems in nothing more likely than in that strange infatuation of hopeless toil which so often possesses them. I have known them in their journeyings ram themselves heroically against rocks, and long abide there, nudging, wriggling, wedging, in order to displace them, and so hold on their inflexible path. Their crowning curse is their drudging impulse to straightforwardness in a belittered world.

Meeting with no such hindrance as their companion did, the other tortoises merely fell foul of small stumbling-blocks – buckets, blocks, and coils of rigging – and at times in the act of crawling over them would slip with an astounding rattle to the deck. Listening to these draggings and concussions, I thought me of the haunt from which they came: an isle full of metallic ravines and gulches, sunk bottomlessly into the hearts of splintered mountains, and covered for many miles with inextricable thickets. I then pictured these three straightforward monsters, century after century, writhing through the shades, grim as blacksmiths, crawling so slowly and ponderously that not only did toadstools and all fungus things grow beneath their feet, but a sooty moss sprouted upon their backs. With them I lost myself in volcanic mazes, brushed away endless boughs of rotting thickets, till finally in a dream I found myself sitting cross-legged upon the foremost, a brahmin similarly mounted upon either side, forming a tripod of foreheads which upheld the universal cope.

Such was the wild nightmare begot by my first impression of the Encantadas tortoise. But next evening, strange to say, I sat down with my shipmates and made a merry repast from tortoise steaks and tortoise stews; and, supper over, out knife, and helped convert the three mighty concave shells into three fanciful soup tureens, and polished the three flat yellowish calipees into three gorgeous salvers.

Sketch Third
Rock Rodondo

For they this hight the Rock of vile Reproach,
A dangerous and dreadful place,
To which nor fish nor fowl did once approach,
But yelling meaws with sea-gulls hoars and bace
And cormoyrants with birds of ravenous race,
Which still sit waiting on that dreadful clift.

With that the rolling sea resounding soft
In his big base them fitly answered,
And on the Rock, the waves breaking aloft,
A solemn meane unto them measured.

Then he the boteman bad row easily,
And let him heare some part of that rare melody.

Suddeinly an innumerable flight
Of harmefull fowles about them fluttering cride,
And with their wicked wings them oft did smight
And sore annoyed, groping in that griesly night.

Even all the nation of unfortunate
And fatal birds about them flocked were.

To go up into a high stone tower is not only a very fine thing in itself, but the very best mode of gaining a comprehensive view of the region round about. It is all the better if this tower stand solitary and alone, like that mysterious Newport one, or else be sole survivor of some perished castle.

Now, with reference to the Enchanted Isles, we are fortunately supplied with just such a noble point of observation in a remarkable rock, from its peculiar figure called of old by the Spaniards, Rock Rodondo, or Round Rock. Some two hundred and fifty feet high, rising straight from the sea ten miles from land, with the whole mountainous group to the south and east, Rock Rodondo occupies, on a large scale, very much the position which the famous Campanile or detached Bell Tower of St Mark does with respect to the tangled group of hoary edifices around it.

Ere ascending, however, to gaze abroad upon the Encantadas, this sea tower itself claims attention. It is visible at the distance of thirty miles, and, fully participating in that enchantment which pervades the group, when first seen afar invariably is mistaken for a sail. Four leagues away, of a golden, hazy noon, it seems some Spanish admiral's ship, stacked up with glittering canvas. 'Sail ho!' 'Sail ho!' 'Sail ho!' from all three masts. But coming nigh, the enchanted frigate is transformed apace into a craggy keep.

My first visit to the spot was made in the grey of the morning. With a view of fishing, we had lowered three boats, and, pulling some two miles from our vessel, found ourselves just before dawn of day close under the moon shadow of Rodondo. Its aspect was heightened, and yet softened, by the strange double twilight of the hour. The great full moon burnt in the low west like a half-spent beacon, casting a soft mellow tinge upon the sea like that cast by a waning fire of embers upon a midnight hearth; while along the entire east the invisible sun sent pallid intimations of his coming. The wind was light, the waves languid; the stars twinkled with a faint effulgence; all nature seemed supine with the long night-watch, and half-suspended in jaded expectation of the sun. This was the critical hour to catch Rodondo in his perfect mood. The twilight was just enough to reveal every striking point, without tearing away the dim investiture of wonder.

From a broken, stair-like base, washed as the steps of a water palace by the waves, the tower rose in entablatures of strata to a shaven summit. These uniform layers, which compose the mass, form its most peculiar feature. For at their lines of junction they project flatly into encircling shelves, from top to bottom, rising one above another in graduated series. And as the eaves of any old barn or abbey are alive with swallows, so were all these rocky ledges with unnumbered sea-fowl. Eaves upon eaves, and nests upon nests. Here and there were long birdlime streaks of a ghostly white staining the tower from sea to air, readily accounting for its sail-like look afar. All would have been bewitchingly quiescent were it not for the demoniac din created by the birds. Not only were the eaves rustling with them, but they flew densely overhead, spreading themselves into a winged and continually shifting canopy. The tower is the resort of aquatic birds for hundreds of leagues around. To the north, to the east, to the west, stretches nothing but eternal ocean; so that the man-of-war hawk coming from the coasts of North America, Polynesia, or Peru, makes his first land at Rodondo. And yet, though Rodondo be terra firma, no land bird ever lighted on it. Fancy a red robin or a canary there! What a falling into the hands of the Philistines, when the poor warbler should be surrounded by such locust-flights of strong bandit birds, with long bills cruel as daggers.

I know not where one can better study the natural history of strange sea-fowl than at Rodondo. It is the aviary of ocean. Birds light here which never touched mast or tree; hermit-birds, which ever fly alone; cloud-birds, familiar with unpierced zones of air.

Let us first glance low down to the lowermost shelf of all, which is the widest, too, and but a little space from high-water mark. What outlandish beings are these? Erect as men, but hardly as symmetrical, they stand all round the rock like sculptured caryatides, supporting the next range of eaves above. Their bodies are grotesquely misshapen, their bills short, their feet seemingly legless; while the members at their sides are neither fin, wing, nor arm. And truly neither fish, flesh, nor fowl is the penguin; as an edible, pertaining neither to Carnival nor Lent; without exception the most ambiguous and least lovely creature yet discovered by man. Though dabbling in all three elements, and indeed possessing some rudimental claims to all, the penguin is at home in none. On land it stumps; afloat it sculls; in the air it flops. As if ashamed of her failure, Nature keeps this ungainly child hidden away at the ends of the earth, in the Straits of Magellan, and on the abased sea-story of Rodondo.

But look, what are yon woebegone regiments drawn up on the next shelf above? What rank and file of large strange fowl? What sea Friars of Orders Grey? Pelicans. Their elongated bills, and heavy leather pouches suspended thereto, give them the most lugubrious expression. A pensive race, they stand for hours together without motion. Their dull, ashy plumage imparts an aspect as if they had been powdered over with cinders. A penitential bird, indeed, fitly haunting the shores of the clinkered Encantadas, whereon tormented Job himself might have well sat down and scraped himself with potsherds.

Higher up now we mark the gony, or grey albatross, anomalously so called, an unsightly, unpoetic bird, unlike its storied kinsman, which is the snow-white ghost of the haunted Capes of Hope and Horn.

As we still ascend from shelf to shelf, we find the tenants of the tower serially disposed in order of their magnitude: gannets, black and speckled haglets, jays, sea hens, sperm-whale birds, gulls of all varieties – thrones, princedoms, powers, dominating one above another in senatorial array – while, sprinkled over all, like an ever-repeated fly in a great piece of embroidery, the stormy petrel or Mother Carey's chicken sounds his continual challenge and alarm. That this mysterious hummingbird of ocean – which, had it but brilliancy of hue, might, from its evanescent liveliness, be almost called its butterfly, yet whose chirrup under the stern is ominous to mariners as to the peasant the death-tick sounding from behind the chimney jamb – should have its special haunt at the Encantadas, contributes, in the seaman's mind, not a little to their dreary spell.

As day advances the dissonant din augments. With ear-splitting cries the wild birds celebrate their matins. Each moment, flights push from the tower and join the aerial choir hovering overhead, while their places below are supplied by darting myriads. But down through all this discord of commotion I hear clear, silver, bugle-like notes unbrokenly falling, like oblique lines of swift-slanting rain in a cascading shower. I gaze far up, and behold a snow-white angelic thing with one long, lance-like feather thrust out behind. It is the bright, inspiriting chanticleer of ocean, the beauteous bird, from its bestirring whistle of musical invocation fitly styled the 'boatswain's mate'.

The winged, life-clouding Rodondo had its full counterpart in the finny hosts which peopled the waters at its base. Below the water-line, the rock seemed one honeycomb of grottos, affording labyrinthine lurking places for swarms of fairy fish. All were strange, many exceedingly beautiful, and would have well graced the costliest glass globes in which goldfish are kept for a show. Nothing was more striking than the complete novelty of many individuals of this multitude. Here hues were seen as yet unpainted, and figures which are unengraved.

To show the multitude, avidity, and nameless fearlessness and tameness of these fish, let me say that often, marking through clear spaces of water – temporarily made so by the concentric dartings of the fish above the surface – certain larger and less unwary wights which swam slow and deep, our anglers would cautiously essay to drop their lines down to these last. But in vain: there was no passing the uppermost zone. No sooner did the hook touch the sea than a hundred infatuates contended for the honour of capture. Poor fish of Rodondo! In your victimised confidence, you are of the number of those who inconsiderately trust, while they do not understand, human nature.

But the dawn is now fairly day. Band after band, the sea-fowl sail away to forage the deep for their food. The tower is left solitary, save the fish-caves at its base. Its birdlime gleams in the golden rays like the whitewash of a tall lighthouse, or the lofty sails of a cruiser. This moment, doubtless, while we know it to be a dead desert rock, other voyagers are taking oaths it is a glad populous ship.

But ropes now, and let us ascend. Yet soft, this is not so easy.

Sketch Fourth
A Pisgah View From the Rock [3]

– That done, he leads him to the highest mount,
From whence far off he unto him did show: –

If you seek to ascend Rock Rodondo, take the following prescription. Go three voyages round the world as a main royal-man of the tallest frigate that floats, then serve a year or two apprenticeship to the guides who conduct strangers up the Peak of Tenerife, and as many more respectively to a rope-dancer, an Indian juggler, and a chamois. This done, come and be rewarded by the view from our tower. How we got there, we alone know. If we sought to tell others, what the wiser were they? Suffice it that here at the summit you and I stand. Does any balloonist, does the outlooking man in the moon, take a broader view of space? Much thus, one fancies, looks the universe from Milton's celestial battlements. A boundless watery Kentucky. Here Daniel Boone[4] would have dwelt content.

Never heed for the present yonder Burnt District of the Enchanted Isles. Look edgeways, as it were, past them, to the south. You see nothing; but permit me to point out the direction, if not the place, of certain interesting objects in the vast sea, which, kissing this tower's base, we behold unscrolling itself towards the Antarctic Pole.

We stand now ten miles from the equator. Yonder, to the east some six hundred miles, lies the continent, this Rock being just about on the parallel of Quito.

Observe another thing here. We are at one of three uninhabited clusters, which, at pretty nearly uniform distances from the main, sentinel, at long intervals from each other, the entire coast of South America. In a peculiar manner, also, they terminate the South American character of country. Of the unnumbered Polynesian chains to the westward, not one partakes of the qualities of the Encantadas or Galapagos, the isles of St Felix and St Ambrose, the isles Juan Fernandez and Massafuero. Of the first, it needs not here to speak. The second lie a little above the Southern Tropic, lofty, inhospitable, and uninhabitable rocks, one of which, presenting two round hummocks connected by a low reef, exactly resembles a huge double-headed shot. The last lie in the latitude of 33 degrees, high, wild and cloven. Juan Fernandez is sufficiently famous without further description. Massafuero is a Spanish name, expressive of the fact that the isle so-called lies *more without*, that is, further off the main than its neighbour Juan. This isle Massafuero has a very imposing aspect at a distance of eight or ten miles. Approached in one direction, in cloudy weather, its great overhanging height and rugged contour, and more especially a peculiar slope of its broad summits, give it much the air of a vast iceberg drifting in tremendous poise. Its sides are split with dark cavernous recesses, as an old cathedral with its gloomy lateral chapels. Drawing nigh one of these gorges from sea, after a long voyage, and beholding some tatterdemalion outlaw, staff in hand, descending its steep rocks toward you, conveys a very queer emotion to a lover of the picturesque.

On fishing parties from ships, at various times, I have chanced to visit each of these groups. The impression they give to the stranger pulling close up in his boat under their grim cliffs is that surely he must be their first discoverer, such, for the most part, is the unimpaired… silence and solitude. And here, by the way, the mode in which these isles were really first lighted upon by Europeans is not unworthy of mention, especially as what is about to be said likewise applies to the original discovery of our Encantadas.

Prior to the year 1563, the voyages made by Spanish ships

from Peru to Chile were full of difficulty. Along this coast, the winds from the south most generally prevail, and it had been an invariable custom to keep close in with the land, from a superstitious conceit on the part of the Spaniards that were they to lose sight of it the eternal trade wind would waft them into unending waters, from whence would be no return. Here, involved among tortuous capes and headlands, shoals and reefs, beating, too, against a continual head wind, often light and sometimes for days and weeks sunk into utter calm, the provincial vessels in many cases suffered the extremest hardships in passages which at the present day seem to have been incredibly protracted. There is on record in some collections of nautical disasters an account of one of these ships, which, starting on a voyage whose duration was estimated at ten days, spent four months at sea, and indeed never again entered harbour, for in the end she was cast away. Singular to tell, this craft never encountered a gale, but was the vexed sport of malicious calms and currents. Thrice, out of provisions, she put back to an intermediate port and started afresh, but only again to return. Frequent fogs enveloped her so that no observation could be had of her place, and once, when all hands were joyously anticipating sight of their destination, lo! the vapours lifted and disclosed the mountains from which they had taken their first departure. In the like deceptive vapours she at last struck upon a reef, whence ensued a long series of calamities too sad to detail.

It was the famous pilot, Juan Fernandez, immortalised by the island named after him, who put an end to these coasting tribulations by boldly venturing the experiment – as De Gama did before him with respect to Europe – of standing broad out from land. Here he found the winds favourable for getting to the south, and by running westward till, beyond the influences of the trades, he regained the coast without difficulty; making the passage which, though in a high degree circuitous, proved far more expeditious than the nominally direct one. Now it was upon these new tracks, and about the year 1670 or thereabouts, that the Enchanted Isles, and the rest of the sentinel groups as they may be called, were discovered. Though I know of no account as to whether any of them were found inhabited or not, it may be reasonably concluded that they had been immemorial solitudes. But let us return to Rodondo.

South-west from our tower lies all Polynesia, hundreds of leagues away; but straight west, on the precise line of his parallel, no land rises till your keel is beached upon the Kingsmills, a nice little sail of, say, five thousand miles.

Having thus by such distant references – with Rodondo the only possible ones – settled our relative place on the sea, let us consider objects not quite so remote. Behold the grim and charred Enchanted Isles. This nearest crater-shaped headland is part of Albemarle, the largest of the group, being some sixty miles or more long, and fifteen broad. Did you ever lay eye on the real genuine equator? Have you ever, in the largest sense, toed the Line? Well, that identical crater-shaped headland there, all yellow lava, is cut by the equator exactly as a knife cuts straight through the centre of a pumpkin pie. If you could only see so far, just to one side of that same headland, across yon low dikey ground, you would catch sight of the isle of Narborough[5], the loftiest land of the cluster; no soil whatsoever, one seamed clinker from top to bottom, abounding in black caves like smithies, its metallic

shore ringing under foot like plates of iron, its central
volcanoes standing grouped like a gigantic chimney-stack.

Narborough and Albemarle are neighbours after a quite
curious fashion. A familiar diagram will illustrate this
strange neighbourhood:

H

Cut a channel at the above letter joint, and the middle
transverse limb is Narborough, and all the rest is Albemarle.
Volcanic Narborough lies in the black jaws of Albemarle
like a wolf's red tongue in his open mouth.

If now you desire the population of Albemarle, I will give
you, in round numbers, the statistics, according to the most
reliable estimates made upon the spot:

Men	.	.	.	.	none
Anteaters	.	.	.	.	unknown
Man-haters	.	.	.	.	unknown
Lizards	.	.	.	.	500,000
Snakes	.	.	.	.	500,000
Spiders	.	.	.	.	10,000,000
Salamanders	.	.	.	.	unknown
Devils	.	.	.	.	unknown
Making a clean total of	.		.	.	11,000,000

exclusive of an incomputable host of fiends, anteaters,
man-haters, and salamanders.

Albemarle opens his mouth towards the setting sun. His
distended jaws form a great bay, which Narborough, his
tongue, divides into halves, one whereof is called Weather

Bay, the other Lee Bay; while the volcanic promontories terminating his coasts are styled south head and north head. I note this because these bays are famous in the annals of the Sperm Whale Fishery. The whales come here at certain seasons to calve. When ships first cruised hereabouts, I am told, they used to blockade the entrance of Lee Bay, when their boats going round by Weather Bay, passed through Narborough channel, and so had the leviathans very neatly in a pen.

The day after we took fish at the base of this Round Tower, we had a fine wind, and shooting round the north headland, suddenly descried a fleet of fully thirty sail, all beating to windward like a squadron in line. A brave sight as ever man saw. A most harmonious concord of rushing keels. Their thirty keelsons hummed like thirty harp-strings, and looked as straight whilst they left their parallel traces on the sea. But there proved too many hunters for the game. The fleet broke up, and went their separate ways out of sight, leaving my own ship and two trim gentlemen of London. These last, finding no luck either, likewise vanished, and Lee Bay, with all its appurtenances, and without a rival, devolved to us.

The way of cruising here is this. You keep hovering about the entrance of the bay, in one beat and out the next. But at times – not always, as in other parts of the group – a racehorse of a current sweeps right across its mouth. So, with all sails set, you carefully ply your tacks. How often, standing at the foremast head at sunrise, with our patient prow pointed in between these isles, did I gaze upon that land, not of cakes, but of clinkers, not of streams of sparkling water, but arrested torrents of tormented lava.

As the ship runs in from the open sea, Narborough presents its side in one dark craggy mass, soaring up some five or six thousand feet, at which point it hoods itself in heavy clouds, whose lowest level fold is as clearly defined against the rocks as the snowline against the Andes. There is dire mischief going on in that upper dark. There toil the demons of fire, who at intervals irradiate the nights with a strange spectral illumination for miles and miles around, but unaccompanied by any further demonstration, or else suddenly announce themselves by terrific concussions and the full drama of a volcanic eruption. The blacker that cloud by day, the more may you look for light by night. Often whalemen have found themselves cruising nigh that burning mountain when all aglow with a ballroom blaze. Or, rather, 'glass works', you may call this same vitreous isle of Narborough, with its tall chimney-stacks.

Where we still stand, here on Rodondo, we cannot see all the other isles, but it is a good place from which to point out where they lie. Yonder, though, to the E.N.E., I mark a distant dusky ridge. It is Abington Isle, one of the most northerly of the group, so solitary, remote, and blank, it looks like no man's land seen off our northern shore. I doubt whether two human beings ever touched upon that spot. So far as yon Abington Isle is concerned, Adam and his billions of posterity remain uncreated.

Ranging south of Abington, and quite out of sight behind the long spine of Albemarle, lies James's Isle, so called by the early buccaneers after the luckless Stuart, Duke of York. Observe here, by the way, that excepting the isles particularised in comparatively recent times, and which mostly received the names of famous admirals, the Encantadas were first christened by the Spaniards; but these Spanish names were generally effaced on English charts by the subsequent christenings of the buccaneers, who, in the middle of the seventeenth century, called them after English noblemen and kings. Of these loyal freebooters and the things which associate their name with the Encantadas, we shall hear anon. Nay, for one little item, immediately, for between James's Isle and Albemarle lies a fantastic islet, strangely known as 'Cowley's Enchanted Isle'[6]. But, as all the group is deemed enchanted, the reason must be given for the spell within a spell involved by this particular designation. The name was bestowed by that excellent buccaneer himself, on his first visit here. Speaking in his published voyages on this spot, he says, 'My fancy led me to call it Cowley's Enchanted Isle, for, we having had a sight of it upon several points of the compass, it appeared always in so many different forms; sometimes like a ruined fortification; upon another point like a great city,' etc. No wonder though that among the Encantadas all sorts of ocular deceptions and mirages should be met.

That Cowley linked his name with this self-transforming and bemocking isle suggests the possibility that it conveyed to him some meditative image of himself. At least, as is not impossible, if he were any relative of the mildly thoughtful and self-upbraiding poet Cowley, who lived about his time, the conceit might seem not unwarranted – for that sort of thing evinced in the naming of this isle runs in the blood, and may be seen in pirates as in poets.

Still south of James's Isle lie Jervis Isle, Duncan Isle, Crossman's Isle, Brattle Isle, Wood's Isle, Chatham Isle and various lesser isles, for the most part an archipelago of aridities, without inhabitant, history, or hope of either in all time to come. But not far from these are rather notable isles – Barrington, Charles's, Norfolk, and Hood's. Succeeding chapters will reveal some ground for their notability.

Sketch Fifth
The Frigate, and Ship Flyaway

Looking far forth into the ocean wide,
A goodly ship with banners bravely dight,
And flag in her top-gallant I espide,
Through the main sea making her merry flight.

Ere quitting Rodondo it must not be omitted that here, in 1813, the US frigate *Essex*, Captain David Porter, came near leaving her bones. Lying becalmed one morning with a strong current setting her rapidly towards the rock, a strange sail was descried, which – not out of keeping with alleged enchantments of the neighbourhood – seemed to be staggering under a violent wind, while the frigate lay lifeless as if spellbound. But a light air springing up, all sail was made by the frigate in chase of the enemy, as supposed – he being deemed an English whale-ship – but the rapidity of the current was so great that soon all sight was lost of him, and at meridian the *Essex*, in spite of her drags, was driven so close under the foam-lashed cliffs of Rodondo that, for a time, all hands gave her up. A smart breeze, however, at last helped her off, though the escape was so critical as to seem almost miraculous.

Thus saved from destruction herself, she now made use of that salvation to destroy the other vessel, if possible. Renewing the chase in the direction in which the stranger had disappeared, sight was caught of him the following morning. Upon being descried he hoisted American colours and stood away from the *Essex*. A calm ensued, when, still confident that the stranger was an Englishman, Porter dispatched a cutter, not to board the enemy, but drive back his boats engaged in towing him. The cutter succeeded. Cutters were subsequently sent to capture him, the stranger now showing English colours in place of American. But when the frigate's boats were within a short distance of their hoped-for prize, another sudden breeze sprang up. The stranger, under all sail, bore off to the westward, and, ere night, was hull down ahead of the *Essex*, which, all this time, lay perfectly becalmed.

This enigmatic craft – American in the morning, and English in the evening, her sails full of wind in a calm – was never again beheld. An enchanted ship, no doubt. So, at least, the sailors swore.

This cruise of the *Essex* in the Pacific during the war of 1812 is, perhaps, the strangest and most stirring to be found in the history of the American navy. She captured the furthest wandering vessels, visited the remotest seas and isles; long hovered in the charmed vicinity of the enchanted group, and, finally, valiantly gave up the ghost fighting two English frigates in the harbour of Valparaiso. Mention is made of her here for the same reason that the buccaneers will likewise receive record: because, like them, by long cruising among the isles, tortoise-hunting upon their shores, and generally exploring them, for these and other reasons, the *Essex* is peculiarly associated with the Encantadas.

Here be it said that you have but three eye-witness authorities worth mentioning touching the Enchanted Isles: Cowley, the buccaneer (1684); Colnet, the whaling-ground explorer (1798); Porter, the post captain (1813). Other than these you have but barren, bootless allusions from some few passing voyagers or compilers.

Sketch Sixth
Barrington Isle and the Buccaneers

Let us all servile base subjection scorn,
And as we be sons of the earth so wide,
Let us our father's heritage divide,
And challenge to ourselves our portions dew
Of all the patrimony, which a few
Now hold on hugger-mugger in their hand.

Lords of the world, and so will wander free,
Whereso us listeth, uncontroll'd of any.

How bravely now we live, how jocund, how near the first
inheritance, without fear, how free from little troubles!

Near two centuries ago Barrington Isle was the resort of that famous wing of the West Indian buccaneers, which, upon their repulse from the Cuban waters, crossing the Isthmus of Darien, ravaged the Pacific side of the Spanish colonies, and, with the regularity and timing of a modern mail, waylaid the royal treasure ships plying between Manila and Acapulco. After the toils of piratic war, here they came to say their prayers, enjoy their free-and-easies, count their crackers from the cask, their doubloons from the keg, and measure their silks of Asia with long Toledos for their yardsticks.

As a secure retreat, an undiscoverable hiding place, no spot in those days could have been better fitted. In the centre of a vast and silent sea but very little traversed, surrounded by islands whose inhospitable aspect might well drive away the chance navigator and yet within a few days' sail of the opulent countries which they made their prey, the unmolested buccaneers found here that tranquillity which they fiercely denied to every civilised harbour in that part of the world. Here, after stress of weather, or a temporary drubbing at the hands of their vindictive foes, or in swift flight with golden booty, those old marauders came, and lay snugly out of all harm's reach. But not only was the place a harbour of safety, and a bower of ease, but for utility in other things it was most admirable.

Barrington Isle is, in many respects, singularly adapted to careening, refitting, refreshing, and other seamen's purposes. Not only has it good water, and good anchorage, well sheltered from all winds by the high land of Albemarle, but it is the least unproductive isle of the group. Tortoises good for food, trees good for fuel, and long grass good for bedding abound here, and there are pretty natural walks, and several landscapes to be seen. Indeed, though in its locality belonging to the Enchanted group, Barrington Isle is so unlike most of its neighbours that it would hardly seem of kin to them.

'I once landed on its western side,' says a sentimental voyager long ago, 'where it faces the black buttress of Albemarle. I walked beneath groves of trees – not very lofty, and not palm trees, or orange trees, or peach trees, to be sure – but, for all that, after long seafaring, very beautiful to walk under, even though they supplied no fruit. And here, in calm spaces at the heads of glades, and on the shaded tops of slopes commanding the most quiet scenery – what do you think I saw? Seats which might have served brahmins and presidents of peace societies. Fine old ruins of what had once been symmetric lounges of stone and turf, they bore every mark both of artificialness and age, and were, undoubtedly, made by the buccaneers. One had been a long sofa with back and arms, just such a sofa as the poet Gray might have loved to throw himself upon, his Crebillon in hand.

'Though they sometimes tarried here for months at a time, and used the spot for a storing place for spare spars, sails, and casks, yet it is highly improbable that the buccaneers ever erected dwelling houses upon the isle. They never were here except their ships remained, and they would most likely have slept on board. I mention this because I cannot avoid the thought that it is hard to impute the construction of these romantic seats to any other motive than one of pure peacefulness and kindly fellowship with nature. That the buccaneers perpetrated the greatest outrages is very true, that some of them were mere cut-throats is not to be denied; but we know that here and there among their host was a Dampier, a Wafer[7], and a Cowley, and likewise other men, whose worst reproach was their desperate fortunes – whom persecution, or adversity, or secret and unavengeable wrongs, had driven from Christian society to seek the melancholy solitude or the guilty adventures of the sea. At any rate, long as those ruins of seats on Barrington remain, the most singular monuments are furnished to the fact that all the buccaneers were not unmitigated monsters.

'But during my ramble on the isle I was not long in discovering other tokens of things quite in accordance with those wild traits, popularly, and no doubt truly enough, imputed to the freebooters at large. Had I picked up old sails and rusty hoops I would only have thought of the ship's carpenter and cooper. But I found old cutlasses and daggers reduced to mere threads of rust, which, doubtless, had stuck between Spanish ribs ere now. These were signs of the murderer and robber; the reveller likewise had left his trace. Mixed with shells, fragments of broken jars were lying here and there, high up upon the beach. They were precisely like the jars now used upon the Spanish coast for the wine and pisco spirits of that country.

'With a rusty dagger fragment in one hand, and a bit of a wine jar in another, I sat me down on the ruinous green sofa I have spoken of and bethought me long and deeply of these same buccaneers. Could it be possible that they robbed and murdered one day, revelled the next, and rested themselves by turning meditative philosophers, rural poets, and seat-builders on the third? Not very improbable, after all. For consider the vacillations of a man. Still, strange as it may seem, I must also abide by the more charitable thought, namely, that among these adventurers were some gentle-manly, companionable souls, capable of genuine tranquillity and virtue.'

Sketch Seventh
Charles's Isle and the Dog-King

– So with outragious cry,
A thousand villeins round about him swarmed
Out of the rocks and caves adjoining nye;
Vile caitive wretches, ragged, rude, deformed;
All threatning death, all in straunge manner armed;
Some with unweldy clubs, some with long speares,
Some rusty knives, some staves in fier warmd.

We will not be of any occupation,
Let such vile vassals, born to base vocation,
Drudge in the world, and for their living droyle,
Which have no wit to live withouten toyle.

South-west of Barrington lies Charles's Isle. And hereby hangs a history which I gathered long ago from a shipmate learned in all the lore of outlandish life.

During the successful revolt of the Spanish provinces from Old Spain, there fought on behalf of Peru a certain Creole adventurer from Cuba who, by his bravery and good fortune, at length advanced himself to high rank in the patriot army. The war being ended, Peru found itself like many valorous gentlemen, free and independent enough, but with few shot in the locker. In other words, Peru had not wherewithal to pay off its troops. But the Creole – I forget his name – volunteered to take his pay in lands. So they told him he might have his pick of the Enchanted Isles, which were then, as they still remain, the nominal appanage of Peru. The soldier straight away embarks thither, explores the group, returns to Callao, and says he will take a deed of Charles's Isle. Moreover, this deed must stipulate that thenceforth Charles's Isle is not only the sole property of the Creole, but is forever free of Peru, even as Peru of Spain. To be short, this adventurer procures himself to be made in effect Supreme Lord of the Island, one of the princes of the powers of the earth.[*]

He now sends forth a proclamation inviting subjects to his as yet unpopulated kingdom. Some eighty souls, men and women, respond, and being provided by their leader with necessaries, and tools of various sorts, together with a

[*] The American Spaniards have long been in the habit of making presents of islands to deserving individuals. The pilot Juan Fernandez procured a deed of the isle named after him, and for some years resided there before Selkirk came. It is supposed, however, that he eventually contracted the blues upon his princely property, for after a time he returned to the main, and as report goes, became a very garrulous barber in the city of Lima.

few cattle and goats, take ship for the promised land, the last arrival on board, prior to sailing, being the Creole himself, accompanied, strange to say, by a disciplined cavalry company of large grim dogs. These, it was observed on the passage, refusing to consort with the emigrants, remained aristocratically grouped around their master on the elevated quarterdeck, casting disdainful glances forward upon the inferior rabble there, much as, from the ramparts, the soldiers of a garrison, thrown into a conquered town, eye the inglorious citizen-mob over which they are set to watch.

Now Charles's Isle not only resembles Barrington Isle in being much more inhabitable than other parts of the group, but it is double the size of Barrington, say forty or fifty miles in circuit.

Safely debarked at last, the company, under direction of their lord and patron, forthwith proceeded to build their capital city. They make considerable advance in the way of walls of clinkers, and lava floors, nicely sanded with cinders. On the least barren hills they pasture their cattle, while the goats, adventurers by nature, explore the far inland solitudes for a scanty livelihood of lofty herbage. Meantime, abundance of fish and tortoises supply their other wants.

The disorders incident to settling all primitive regions in the present case were heightened by the peculiarly untoward character of many of the pilgrims. His Majesty was forced at last to proclaim martial law and actually hunted and shot with his own hand several of his rebellious subjects who, with most questionable intentions, had clandestinely encamped in the interior, whence they stole by night, to prowl barefooted on tiptoe round the precincts of the lava palace. It is to be remarked, however, that prior to such stern proceedings, the more reliable men had been judiciously picked out for an infantry bodyguard, subordinate to the cavalry bodyguard of dogs. But the state of politics in this unhappy nation may be somewhat imagined from the circumstance that all who were not of the bodyguard were downright plotters and malignant traitors. At length the death penalty was tacitly abolished, owing to the timely thought that, were strict sportsman's justice to be dispensed among such subjects, ere long the Nimrod King would have little or no remaining game to shoot. The human part of the lifeguard was now disbanded and set to work cultivating the soil and raising potatoes, the regular army now solely consisting of the dog-regiment. These, as I have heard, were of a singularly ferocious character, though by severe training rendered docile to their master. Armed to the teeth, the Creole now goes in state, surrounded by his canine janizaries, whose terrific bayings prove quite as serviceable as bayonets in keeping down the surgings of revolt.

But the census of the isle, sadly lessened by the dispensation of justice, and not materially recruited by matrimony, began to fill his mind with sad mistrust. Some way the population must be increased. Now, from its possessing a little water, and its comparative pleasantness of aspect, Charles's Isle at this period was occasionally visited by foreign whalers. These His Majesty had always levied upon for port charges, thereby contributing to his revenue. But now he had additional designs. By insidious arts he from time to time cajoles certain sailors to desert their ships and enlist beneath his banner. Soon as missed, their captains crave permission to go and hunt them up. Whereupon His Majesty first hides them very carefully away, and then freely permits the search. In consequence, the delinquents are never found, and the ships retire without them.

Thus, by a two-edged policy of this crafty monarch, foreign nations were crippled in the number of their subjects, and his own were greatly multiplied. He particularly petted these renegade strangers. But alas for the deep-laid schemes of ambitious princes, and alas for the vanity of glory. As the foreign-born Pretorians – unwisely introduced into the Roman state, and still more unwisely made favourites of the emperors – at last insulted and overturned the throne, even so these lawless mariners, with all the rest of the bodyguard and all the populace, broke out into a terrible mutiny, and defied their master. He marched against them with all his dogs. A deadly battle ensued upon the beach. It raged for three hours, the dogs fighting with determined valour, and the sailors reckless of everything but victory. Three men and thirteen dogs were left dead upon the field, many on both sides were wounded, and the king was forced to fly with the remainder of his canine regiment. The enemy pursued, stoning the dogs with their master into the wilderness of the interior. Discontinuing the pursuit, the victors returned to the village on the shore, stove the spirit casks, and proclaimed a republic. The dead men were interred with the honour of war, and the dead dogs ignominiously thrown into the sea.

At last, forced by stress of suffering, the fugitive Creole came down from the hills and offered to treat for peace. But the rebels refused it on any other terms than his unconditional banishment. Accordingly, the next ship that arrived recarried away the ex-king to Peru.

The history of the King of Charles's Island furnishes another illustration of the difficulty of colonising barren islands with unprincipled pilgrims.

Doubtless for a long time the exiled monarch, pensively ruralising in Peru, which afforded him a safe asylum in his calamity, watched every arrival from the Encantadas, to hear news of the failure of the republic, the consequent penitence of the rebels, and his own recall to royalty. Doubtless he deemed the republic but a miserable experiment which would soon explode. But no, the insurgents had confederated themselves into a democracy neither Grecian, Roman, nor American. Nay, it was no democracy at all, but a permanent *riotocracy*, which gloried in having no law but lawlessness. Great inducements being offered to deserters, their ranks were swelled by accessions of scamps from every ship which touched their shores. Charles's Island was proclaimed the asylum of the oppressed of all navies. Each runaway tar was hailed as a martyr in the cause of freedom, and became immediately installed a ragged citizen of this universal nation. In vain the captains of absconding seamen strove to regain them. Their new compatriots were ready to give any number of ornamental eyes on their behalf. They had few cannon, but their fists were not to be trifled with. So at last it came to pass that no vessels acquainted with the character of that country durst touch there, however sorely in want of refreshment. It became anathema – a sea Alsatia – the unassailed lurking place of all sorts of desperadoes, who in the name of liberty did just what they pleased. They continually fluctuated in their numbers. Sailors, deserting ships at other islands, or in boats at sea anywhere in that vicinity, steered for Charles's Isle as to their sure home of refuge; while, sated with the life of the isle, numbers from time to time crossed the water to the neighbouring ones and there presenting themselves to strange captains as ship-wrecked seamen often succeeded in getting on board vessels bound to the Spanish coast, and having a com-passionate purse made up for them on landing there.

One warm night during my first visit to the group, our ship was floating along in languid stillness when someone on the forecastle shouted: 'Light ho!' We looked and saw a beacon burning on some obscure land off the beam. Our third mate was not intimate with this part of the world. Going to the captain he said, 'Sir, shall I put off in a boat? These must be shipwrecked men.'

The captain laughed rather grimly, as, shaking his fist towards the beacon, he rapped out an oath, and said, 'No, no, you precious rascals, you don't juggle one of my boats ashore this blessed night. You do well, you thieves – you do benevolently to hoist a light yonder as on a dangerous shoal. It tempts no wise man to pull off and see what's the matter, but bids them steer small and keep off shore – that is Charles's Island; brace up, Mr Mate, and keep the light astern.'

Sketch Eighth
Norfolk Isle and the Chola Widow

At last they in an island did espy
A seemly woman sitting by the shore,
That with great sorrow and sad agony
Seemed some great misfortune to deplore,
And loud to them for succor called evermore.

Black his eye as the midnight sky,
White his neck as the driven snow,
Red his cheek as the morning light; –
Cold he lies in the ground below.
    My love is dead,
    Gone to his death-bed, ys
All under the cactus tree.

Each lonely scene shall thee restore,
For thee the tear be duly shed;
Belov'd till life can charm no more,
And mourned till Pity's self be dead.

Far to the north-east of Charles's Isle, sequestered from the rest, lies Norfolk Isle, and, however insignificant to most voyagers, to me, through sympathy, that lone island has become a spot made sacred by the strangest trials of humanity.

It was my first visit to the Encantadas. Two days had been spent ashore in hunting tortoises. There was not time to capture many, so on the third afternoon we loosed our sails. We were just in the act of getting under way, the uprooted anchor yet suspended and invisibly swaying beneath the wave, as the good ship gradually turned her heel to leave the isle behind, when the seaman who heaved with me at the windlass paused suddenly and directed my attention to something moving on the land, not along the beach, but somewhat back, fluttering from a height.

In view of the sequel of this little story, be it here narrated how it came to pass that an object which partly from its being so small was quite lost to every other man on board, still caught the eye of my handspike companion. The rest of the crew, myself included, merely stood up to our spikes in heaving, whereas, unwontedly exhilarated, at every turn of the ponderous windlass, my belted comrade leapt atop of it, with might and main giving a downward, thewy, perpendicular heave, his raised eye bent in cheery animation upon the slowly receding shore. Being high lifted above all others was the reason he perceived the object, otherwise unperceivable; and this elevation of his eye was owing to the elevation of his spirits; and this again – for truth must out – to a dram of Peruvian pisco, in guerdon for some kindness done, secretly administered to him that morning by our mulatto steward. Now, certainly, pisco does a deal of mischief in the world; yet seeing that, in the present case, it was the means, though indirect, of rescuing a human being from the most dreadful fate, must we not also needs admit that sometimes pisco does a deal of good?

Glancing across the water in the direction pointed out, I saw some white thing hanging from an inland rock, perhaps half a mile from the sea.

'It is a bird, a white-winged bird, perhaps a… no; it is… it is a handkerchief!'

'Aye, a handkerchief!' echoed my comrade, and with a louder shout apprised the captain.

Quickly now – like the running out and training of a great gun – the long cabin spyglass was thrust through the mizen-rigging from the high platform of the poop, whereupon a human figure was plainly seen upon the inland rock, eagerly waving towards us what seemed to be the handkerchief.

Our captain was a prompt, good fellow. Dropping the glass, he lustily ran forward, ordering the anchor to be dropped again, hands to stand by a boat, and lower away.

In a half-hour's time the swift boat returned. It went with six and came with seven; and the seventh was a woman.

It is not with artistic heartlessness, but I wish I could but draw in crayons, for this woman was a most touching sight, and crayons, tracing softly melancholy lines, would best depict the mournful image of the dark-damasked Chola widow.

Her story was soon told, and though given in her own strange language was as quickly understood, for our captain, from long trading on the Chilean coast, was well versed in the Spanish. A Chola, or half-breed Indian woman, of Paita in Peru, three years gone by, with her young new-wedded husband Felipe, of pure Castilian blood, and her one only Indian brother, Truxill, Hunilla had taken passage on the main in a French whaler, commanded by a joyous man, which vessel, bound to the cruising grounds beyond the Enchanted Isles, proposed passing close by their vicinity. The object of the little party was to procure tortoise oil, a fluid which for its great purity and delicacy is held in high estimation wherever known, and it is well-known all along this part of the Pacific coast. With a chest of clothes, tools, cooking utensils, a rude apparatus for trying out the oil, some casks of biscuit, and other things, not omitting two favourite dogs, of which faithful animal all the Cholos are very fond, Hunilla and her companions were safely landed at their chosen place. The Frenchman, according to the contract made ere sailing, engaged to take them off upon returning from a four months' cruise in the westward seas, which interval the three adventurers deemed quite sufficient for their purposes.

On the isle's lone beach they paid him in silver for their passage out, the stranger having declined to carry them at all except upon that condition; though willing to take every means to ensure the due fulfilment of his promise. Felipe had striven hard to have this payment put off to the period of the ship's return. But in vain. Still they thought they had, in another way, ample pledge of the good faith of the Frenchman. It was arranged that the expenses of the passage home should not be payable in silver, but in tortoises – one hundred tortoises ready captured to the returning captain's hand. These the Cholos meant to secure after their own work was done, against the probable time of the Frenchman's coming back, and no doubt in prospect already felt that in those hundred tortoises – now somewhere ranging the isle's interior – they possessed one hundred hostages. Enough: the vessel sailed; the gazing three on shore answered the loud glee of the singing crew; and, ere evening, the French craft was hull down in the distant sea, its masts three faintest lines which quickly faded from Hunilla's eye.

The stranger had given a blithesome promise, and anchored it with oaths, but oaths and anchors equally will drag; naught else abides on fickle earth but unkept promises of joy. Contrary winds from out unstable skies, or contrary moods of his more varying mind, or shipwreck and sudden death in solitary waves – whatever was the cause, the blithe stranger never was seen again.

Yet, however dire a calamity was here in store, misgivings of it ere due time never disturbed the Cholos' busy mind, now all intent upon the toilsome matter which had brought them hither. Nay, by swift doom coming like the thief at night, ere seven weeks went by, two of the little party were removed from all anxieties of land or sea. No more they sought to gaze with feverish fear, or still more feverish hope, beyond the present's horizon line, but into the furthest future their own silent spirits sailed. By persevering labour beneath that burning sun, Felipe and Truxill had brought down to their hut many scores of tortoises, and tried out the oil, when, elated with their good success, and to reward themselves for such hard work, they too hastily made a catamaran, or Indian raft, much used on the Spanish main, and merrily started on a fishing trip, just without a long reef with many jagged gaps, running parallel with the shore, about half a mile from it. By some bad tide or hap, or natural negligence of joyfulness (for though they could not be heard, yet by their gestures they seemed singing all the time) forced in deep water against that iron bar, the ill-made catamaran was overset, and came all to pieces, when, dashed by broad-cheated swells between their broken logs and the sharp teeth of the reef, both adventurers perished before Hunilla's eyes.

Before Hunilla's eyes they sank. The real woe of this event passed before her sight as some sham tragedy on the stage. She was seated on a rude bower among the withered thickets crowning a lofty cliff, a little back from the beach. The thickets were so disposed that in looking upon the sea at large she peered out from among the branches as from the lattice of a high balcony. But upon the day we speak of here, the better to watch the adventure of those two hearts she loved, Hunilla had withdrawn the branches to one side, and held them so. They formed an oval frame, through which the bully boundless sea rolled like a painted one. And there the invisible painter painted to her view the wave-tossed and disjointed raft, its once level logs slantingly upheaved, as raking masts, and the four struggling arms undistinguishable among them, and then all subsided into smooth-flowing creamy waters, slowly drifting the splintered wreck, while, first and last, no sound of any sort was heard. Death in a silent picture, a dream of the eye, such vanishing shapes as the mirage shows.

So instant was the scene, so trancelike its mild pictorial effect, so distant from her blasted bower and her common sense of things, that Hunilla gazed and gazed, nor raised a finger or a wail. But as good to sit thus dumb, in stupor staring on that dumb show, for all that otherwise might be done. With half a mile of sea between, how could her two enchanted arms aid those four fated ones? The distance long, the time one sand. After the lightning is beheld, what fool shall stay the thunderbolt? Felipe's body was washed ashore, but Truxill's never came, only his gay, braided hat of golden straw – that same sunflower thing he waved to her, pushing from the strand – and now, to the last gallant, it still saluted her. But Felipe's body floated to the marge, with one arm encirclingly outstretched. Lockjawed in grim death, the lover-husband softly clasped his bride, true to her even in death's dream. Ah, heaven, when man thus keeps his faith, wilt thou be faithless who created the faithful one? But they cannot break faith who never plighted it.

It needs not to be said what nameless misery now wrapped the lonely widow. In telling her own story she passed this almost entirely over, simply recounting the event. Construe the comment of her features as you might, from her mere words little would you have weened that Hunilla was herself the heroine of her tale. But not thus did she defraud us of our tears. All hearts bled that grief could be so brave.

She but showed us her soul's lid, and the strange ciphers thereon engraved – all within, with pride's timidity, was withheld. Yet was there one exception. Holding out her small olive hand before her captain, she said in mild and slowest Spanish, '*Señor*, I buried him,' then paused, struggled as against the writhed coilings of a snake, and, cringing suddenly, leapt up, repeating in impassioned pain, 'I buried him, my life, my soul!'

Doubtless it was by half-unconscious, automatic motions of her hands that this heavy-hearted one performed the final office for Felipe, and planted a rude cross of withered sticks – no green ones might be had – at the head of that lonely grave where rested now in lasting uncomplaint and quiet haven he whom untranquil seas had overthrown.

But some dull sense of another body that should be interred, of another cross that should hallow another grave – unmade as yet – some dull anxiety and pain touching her undiscovered brother, now haunted the oppressed Hunilla. Her hands fresh from the burial earth, she slowly went back to the beach, with unshaped purposes wandering there, her spellbound eye bent upon the incessant waves. But they bore nothing to her but a dirge which maddened her to think that murderers should mourn. As time went by, and these things came less dreamingly to her mind, the strong persuasions of her Romish faith, which sets peculiar store by consecrated urns, prompted her to resume in waking earnest that pious search which had but begun as in somnambulism. Day after day, week after week, she trod the cindery beach, till at length a double motive edged every eager glance. With equal longing she now looked for the living and the dead – the brother and the captain – alike vanished, never to return. Little accurate note of time had Hunilla taken under such emotions as were hers, and little, outside herself, served for calendar or dial. As to poor Crusoe in the selfsame sea, no saint's bell pealed forth the lapse of week or month; each day went by unchallenged; no chanticleer announced those sultry dawns, no lowing herds those poisonous nights. All wonted and steadily recurring sounds, human, or humanised by sweet fellowship with man, but one stirred that torrid trance – the cry of dogs, save which naught but the rolling sea invaded it, an all-pervading monotone, and to the widow that was the least loved voice she could have heard.

No wonder that, as her thoughts now wandered to the unreturning ship and were beaten back again, the hope against hope so struggled in her soul that at length she desperately said, 'Not yet, not yet; my foolish heart runs on too fast.' So she forced patience for some further weeks. But to those whom earth's sure indraught draws, patience or impatience is still the same.

Hunilla now sought to settle precisely in her mind, to an hour, how long it was since the ship had sailed, and then, with the same precision, how long a space remained to pass. But this proved impossible. What present day or month it was she could not say. Time was her labyrinth in which Hunilla was entirely lost.

And now follows –

Against my own purposes a pause descends upon me here. One knows not whether nature doth not impose some secrecy upon him who has been privy to certain things. At least, it is to be doubted whether it be good to blazon such. If some books are deemed most baneful and their sale forbid, how, then, with deadlier facts, not dreams of doting men? Those whom books will hurt will not be proof against events. Events, not books, should be forbidden. But in all things man sows upon the wind which bloweth just there whither it listeth; for ill or good, man cannot know. Often ill comes from the good, as good from ill.

When Hunilla –

Dire sight it is to see some silken beast long dally with a golden lizard ere she devour. More terrible to see how feline Fate will sometimes dally with a human soul, and by a nameless magic make it repulse a sane despair with a hope which is but mad. Unwittingly I imp this cat-like thing, sporting with the heart of him who reads, for if he feel not he reads in vain.

'The ship sails this day, today,' at last said Hunilla to herself; 'this gives me certain time to stand on; without certainty I go mad. In loose ignorance I have hoped and hoped; now in firm knowledge I will but wait. Now I live and no longer perish in bewilderings. Holy Virgin, aid me! Thou wilt waft back the ship. Oh, past length of weary weeks – all to be dragged over – to buy the certainty of today, I freely give ye, though I tear ye from me!'

As mariners, tossed in tempest on some desolate ledge, patch them a boat out of the remnants of their vessel's wreck, and launch it in the selfsame waves, see here Hunilla, this lone shipwrecked soul, out of treachery invoking trust. Humanity, thou strong thing, I worship thee, not in the laurelled victor, but in this vanquished one.

Truly Hunilla leaned upon a reed, a real one – no metaphor; a real Eastern reed. A piece of hollow cane, drifted from unknown isles, and found upon the beach, its once jagged ends rubbed smoothly even as by sandpaper, its golden glazing gone. Long ground between the sea and land, upper and nether stone, the unvarnished substance was filed bare, and wore another polish now, one with itself, the polish of its agony. Circular lines at intervals cut all round this surface divided it into six panels of unequal length. In the first were scored the days, each tenth one marked by a longer and deeper notch. The second was scored for the number of sea-fowl eggs for sustenance, picked out from the rocky nests. The third, how many fish had been caught from the shore. The fourth, how many small tortoises found inland. The fifth, how many days of sun; the sixth, of clouds – which last, of the two, was the greater one. Long night of busy numbering, misery's mathematics, to weary her too-wakeful soul to sleep, yet sleep for that was none.

The panel of the days was deeply worn – the long tenth notches half effaced, as alphabets of the blind. Ten thousand times the longing widow had traced her finger over the bamboo – dull flute, which, played on, gave no sound – as if counting birds flown by in air would hasten tortoises creeping through the woods.

After the one hundred and eightieth day no further mark was seen; that last one was the faintest, as the first the deepest.

'There were more days,' said our captain; 'Many, many more; why did you not go on and notch them too, Hunilla?'

'*Señor*, ask me not.'

'And meantime, did no other vessel pass the isle?'

'Nay, *señor*, but –'

'You do not speak; but *what*, Hunilla?'

'Ask me not, *señor*.'

'You saw ships pass, far away. You waved to them; they passed on – was that it, Hunilla?'

'*Señor*, be it as you say.'

Braced against her woe, Hunilla would not, durst not, trust the weakness of her tongue. Then when our captain asked whether any whaleboats had –

But no, I will not file this thing complete for scoffing souls to quote, and call it firm proof upon their side. The half shall here remain untold. Those two unnamed events

66

which befell Hunilla on this isle, let them abide between her and her God. In nature, as in law, it may be libellous to speak some truths.

Still, how it was that, although our vessel had lain three days anchored nigh the isle, its one human tenant should not have discovered us till just upon the point of sailing, never to revisit so lone and far a spot, this needs explaining ere the sequel come.

The place where the French captain had landed the little party was on the further and opposite end of the isle. There too it was that they had afterwards built their hut. Nor did the widow in her solitude desert the spot where her loved ones had dwelt with her, and where the dearest of the twain now slept his last long sleep, and all her plaints awaked him not, and he of husbands the most faithful during life.

Now, high broken land rises between the opposite extremities of the isle. A ship anchored at one side is invisible from the other. Neither is the isle so small but a considerable company might wander for days through the wilderness of one side and never be seen, or their halloos heard, by any stranger holding aloof on the other. Hence Hunilla, who naturally associated the possible coming of ships with her own part of the isle, might to the end have remained quite ignorant of the presence of our vessel were it not for a mysterious presentiment borne to her, so our mariners averred, by this isle's enchanted air. Nor did the widow's answer undo the thought.

'How did you come to cross the isle this morning, then, Hunilla?' said our captain.

'*Señor*, something came flitting by me. It touched my cheek, my heart, *señor*.'

'What do you say, Hunilla?'

'I have said, *señor*, something came through the air.'

It was a narrow chance. For when in crossing the isle Hunilla gained the high land in the centre, she must then for the first have perceived our masts, and also marked that their sails were being loosed, perhaps even heard the echoing chorus of the windlass song. The strange ship was about to sail, and she behind. With all haste she now descends the height on the hither side, but soon loses sight of the ship among the sunken jungles at the mountain's base. She struggles on through the withered branches, which seek at every step to bar her path, till she comes to the isolated rock, still some way from the water. This she climbs, to reassure herself. The ship is still in plainest sight. But now, worn out with over-tension, Hunilla all but faints; she fears to step down from her giddy perch; she is fain to pause there where she is, and as a last resort catches the turban from her head, unfurls and waves it over the jungles towards us.

During the telling of her story the mariners formed a voiceless circle round Hunilla and the captain, and when at length the word was given to man the fastest boat and pull round to the isle's thither side, to bring away Hunilla's chest and the tortoise oil, such alacrity of both cheery and sad obedience seldom before was seen. Little ado was made. Already the anchor had been recommitted to the bottom, and the ship swung calmly to it.

But Hunilla insisted upon accompanying the boat as indispensable pilot to her hidden hut. So being refreshed with the best the steward could supply, she started with us. Nor did ever any wife of the most famous admiral, in her husband's barge, receive more silent reverence of respect than poor Hunilla from this boat's crew.

Rounding many a vitreous cape and bluff, in two hours' time we shot inside the fatal reef, wound into a secret cove, looked up along a green many-gabled lava wall, and saw the island's solitary dwelling.

It hung upon an impending cliff, sheltered on two sides by tangled thickets and half-screened from view in front by juttings of the rude stairway which climbed the precipice from the sea. Built of canes, it was thatched with long, mildewed grass. It seemed an abandoned hayrick whose haymakers were now no more. The roof inclined but one way, the eaves coming to within two feet of the ground. And here was a simple apparatus to collect the dews, or rather doubly-distilled and finest winnowed rains which, in mercy or in mockery, the night skies sometimes drop upon these blighted Encantadas. All along beneath the eaves a spotted sheet, quite weather-stained, was spread, pinned to short, upright stakes set in the shallow sand. A small clinker thrown into the cloth weighed its middle down, thereby straining all moisture into a calabash placed below. This vessel supplied each drop of water ever drunk upon the isle by the Cholos. Hunilla told us the calabash would sometimes, but not often, be half filled overnight. It held six quarts, perhaps. 'But,' said she, 'we were used to thirst. At sandy Paita, where I live, no shower from heaven ever fell; all the water there is brought on mules from the inland vales.'

Tied among the thickets were some twenty moaning tortoises, supplying Hunilla's lonely larder while hundreds of vast tabled black bucklers, like displaced, shattered tombstones of dark slate, were also scattered round. These were the skeleton backs of those great tortoises from which Felipe and Truxill had made their precious oil. Several large calabashes and two goodly kegs were filled with it. In a pot nearby were the caked crusts of a quantity which had been permitted to evaporate. 'They meant to have strained it off next day,' said Hunilla, as she turned aside.

I forgot to mention the most singular sight of all, though the first that greeted us after landing.

Some ten small, soft-haired, ringleted dogs of a beautiful breed peculiar to Peru set up a concert of glad welcomings when we gained the beach, which was responded to by Hunilla. Some of these dogs had, since her widowhood, been born upon the isle, the progeny of the two brought from Paita. Owing to the jagged steeps and pitfalls, tortuous thickets, sunken clefts, and perilous intricacies of all sorts in the interior, Hunilla, admonished by the loss of one favourite among them, never allowed these delicate creatures to follow her in her occasional birds' nests climbs and other wanderings; so that, through long habituation, they offered not to follow when that morning she crossed the land, and her own soul was then too full of other things to heed their lingering behind. Yet, all along she had so clung to them that, besides what moisture they lapped up at early daybreak from the small scoop holes among the adjacent rocks, she had shared the dew of her calabash among them, never laying by any considerable store against those prolonged and utter droughts which, in some disastrous seasons, warp these isles.

Having pointed out, at our desire, what few things she would like transported to the ship – her chest, the oil, not omitting the live tortoises which she intended for a grateful present to our captain – we immediately set to work, carrying them to the boat down the long, sloping stair of deeply shadowed rock. While my comrades were thus employed, I looked, and Hunilla had disappeared.

It was not curiosity alone, but, it seems to me, something different mingled with it which prompted me to drop my tortoise and once more gaze slowly around. I remembered the husband buried by Hunilla's hands. A narrow pathway led into a dense part of the thickets. Following it through many mazes, I came out upon a small round open space, deeply chambered there.

The mound rose in the middle; a bare heap of finest sand, like that unverdured heap found at the bottom of an hourglass run out. At its head stood the cross of withered sticks, the dry, peeled bark still fraying from it, its transverse limb tied up with rope and forlornly adroop in the silent air.

Hunilla was partly prostrate upon the grave, her dark head bowed, and lost in her long, loosened Indian hair, her hands extended to the cross-foot with a little brass crucifix clasped between – a crucifix worn featureless, like an ancient graven knocker long plied in vain. She did not see me, and I made no noise, but slid aside and left the spot.

A few moments ere all was ready for our going, she reappeared among us. I looked into her eyes, but saw no tear. There was something which seemed strangely haughty in her air, and yet it was the air of woe. A Spanish and an Indian grief, which would not visibly lament. Pride's height in vain abased to proneness on the rack; nature's pride subduing nature's torture.

Like pages the small and silken dogs surrounded her as she slowly descended towards the beach. She caught the two most eager creatures in her arms: 'Mia Teeta! Mia Tomoteeta!' and, fondling them, enquired how many could we take on board.

The mate commanded the boat's crew – not a hard-hearted man, but his way of life had been such that in most things, even in the smallest, simple utility was his leading motive.

'We cannot take them all, Hunilla; our supplies are short; the winds are unreliable; we may be a good many days going to Tombez. So take those you have, Hunilla, but no more.'

She was in the boat; the oarsmen, too, were seated; all save one, who stood ready to push off and then spring himself. With the sagacity of their race, the dogs now seemed aware that they were in the very instant of being deserted upon a barren strand. The gunwales of the boat were high; its prow – presented inland – was lifted; so, owing to the water, which they seemed instinctively to shun, the dogs could not well leap into the little craft. But their busy paws hard scraped the prow, as it had been some farmer's door shutting them out from shelter in a winter storm. A clamorous agony of alarm. They did not howl, or whine; they all but spoke.

'Push off! Give way!' cried the mate. The boat gave one heavy drag and lurch, and next moment shot swiftly from the beach, turned on her heel, and sped. The dogs ran howling along the water's marge, now pausing to gaze at the flying boat, then motioning as if to leap in chase, but mysteriously withheld themselves, and again ran howling along the beach. Had they been human beings, hardly would they have more vividly inspired the sense of desolation. The oars were plied as confederate feathers of two wings. No one spoke. I looked back upon the beach, and then upon Hunilla, but her face was set in a stern dusky calm. The dogs crouching in her lap vainly licked her rigid hands. She never looked behind her, but sat motionless till we turned a promontory of the coast and lost all sights and sounds astern. She seemed as one who, having experienced the sharpest of mortal pangs, was henceforth content to have all lesser heart-strings riven, one by one. To Hunilla, pain seemed so necessary that pain in other beings, though by love and sympathy made her own, was unrepiningly to be borne. A heart of yearning in a frame of steel. A heart of earthy yearning, frozen by the frost which falleth from the sky.

The sequel is soon told. After a long passage, vexed by calms and baffling winds, we made the little port of Tombez in Peru, there to recruit the ship. Paita was not very distant. Our captain sold the tortoise oil to a Tombez merchant, and adding to the silver a contribution from all hands, gave it to our silent passenger who knew not what the mariners had done.

The last seen of lone Hunilla she was passing into Paita town, riding upon a small grey ass, and before her on the ass' shoulders she eyed the jointed workings of the beast's armorial cross.

Sketch Ninth
Hood's Isle and the Hermit Oberlus[8]

That darkesome glen they enter, where they find
That cursed man low sitting on the ground,
Musing full sadly in his sullein mind;
His griesly lockes long grouen and unbound,
Disordered hong about his shoulders round,
And hid his face, through which his hollow eyne
Lookt deadly dull, and stared as astound;
His raw-bone cheekes, through penurie and pine,
Were shronke into the jawes, as he did never dine.
His garments nought but many ragged clouts,
With thornes together pind and patched reads,
The which his naked sides he wrapt abouts.

South-east of Crossman's Isle lies Hood's Isle, or McCain's Beclouded Isle, and upon its south side is a vitreous cove with a wide strand of dark pounded black lava, called Black Beach, or Oberlus's Landing. It might fitly have been styled Charon's.

It received its name from a wild white creature who spent many years here, in the person of a European bringing into this savage region qualities more diabolical than are to be found among any of the surrounding cannibals.

About half a century ago, Oberlus deserted at the above-named island, then, as now, a solitude. He built himself a den of lava and clinkers, about a mile from the landing, subsequently called after him, in a vale or expanded gulch, containing here and there among the rocks about two acres of soil capable of rude cultivation, the only place on the isle not too blasted for that purpose. Here he succeeded in raising a sort of degenerate potatoes and pumpkins, which from time to time he exchanged with needy whalemen passing, for spirits or dollars.

His appearance from all accounts was that of the victim of some malignant sorceress; he seemed to have drunk of Circe's cup; beastlike; rags insufficient to hide his naked-ness; his befreckled skin blistered by continual exposure to the sun; nose flat; countenance contorted, heavy, earthy; hair and beard unshorn, profuse, and of fiery red. He struck strangers much as if he were a volcanic creature thrown up by the same convulsion which exploded into sight the isle. All bepatched and coiled asleep in his lonely lava den among the mountains, he looked, they say, as a heaped drift of withered leaves, torn from autumn trees, and so left in some hidden nook by the whirling halt for an instant of a fierce night wind, which then ruthlessly sweeps on, some-where else to repeat the capricious act. It is also reported to have been the strangest sight, this same Oberlus, of a sultry, cloudy morning, hidden under his shocking old black tarpaulin hat, hoeing potatoes among the lava. So warped and crooked was his strange nature that the very handle of his hoe seemed gradually to have shrunk and twisted in his grasp, being a wretched bent stick, elbowed more like a savage's war sickle than a civilised hoe handle. It was his mysterious custom upon a first encounter with a stranger ever to present his back, possibly because that was his better side, since it revealed the least. If the encounter chanced in his garden, as it sometimes did – the new-landed strangers going from the seaside straight through the gorge to hunt up the queer greengrocer reported doing business here – Oberlus for a time hoed on, unmindful of all greeting, jovial or bland, as the curious stranger would turn to face him, the recluse, hoe in hand, as diligently would avert himself, bowed over, and sullenly revolving round his murphy hill. Thus far for hoeing. When planting, his whole aspect and all his gestures were so malevolently and use-lessly sinister and secret that he seemed rather in act of dropping poison into wells than potatoes into soil. But among his lesser and more harmless marvels was an idea he ever had that his visitors came equally as well led by long-ings to behold the mighty hermit Oberlus in his royal state of solitude as simply to obtain potatoes, or find whatever company might be upon a barren isle. It seems incredible that such a being should possess such vanity, a misanthrope be conceited; but he really had his notion, and, upon the strength of it, often gave himself amusing airs to captains.

But after all this is somewhat of a piece with the well-known eccentricity of some convicts, proud of that very hatefulness which makes them notorious. At other times another unaccountable whim would seize him, and he would long dodge advancing strangers round the clinkered corners of his hut; sometimes, like a stealthy bear, he would slink through the withered thickets up the mountains and refuse to see the human face.

Except his occasional visitors from the sea, for a long period the only companions of Oberlus were the crawling tortoises, and he seemed more than degraded to their level, having no desires for a time beyond theirs, unless it were for the stupor brought on by drunkenness. But, sufficiently debased as he appeared, there yet lurked in him, only awaiting occasion for discovery, a still further proneness. Indeed, the sole superiority of Oberlus over the tortoises was his possession of a larger capacity of degradation, and, along with that, something like an intelligent will to it. Moreover, what is about to be revealed perhaps will show that selfish ambition, or the love of rule for its own sake, far from being the peculiar infirmity of noble minds, is shared by beings which have no mind at all. No creatures are so selfishly tyrannical as some brutes, as anyone who has observed the tenants of the pasture must occasionally have observed.

'This island's mine by Sycorax my mother,' said Oberlus to himself, glaring round upon his haggard solitude. By some means, barter or theft – for in those days ships at intervals still kept touching at his landing – he obtained an old musket, with a few charges of powder and ball. Possessed of arms, he was stimulated to enterprise, as a tiger that first feels the coming of its claws. The long habit of sole dominion over every object round him, his almost unbroken solitude, his never encountering humanity except on terms of misanthropic independence or mercantile craftiness, and even such encounters being comparatively but rare – all this must have gradually nourished in him a vast idea of his own importance, together with a pure animal sort of scorn for all the rest of the universe.

The unfortunate Creole who enjoyed his brief term of royalty at Charles's Isle was perhaps in some degree influenced by not unworthy motives such as prompt other adventurous spirits to lead colonists into distant regions and assume political pre-eminence over them. His summary execution of many of his Peruvians is quite pardonable considering the desperate characters he had to deal with, while his offering canine battle to the banded rebels seems under the circumstances altogether just. But for this King Oberlus and what shortly follows, no shade of palliation can be given. He acted out of mere delight in tyranny and cruelty, by virtue of a quality in him inherited from Sycorax his mother. Armed now with that shocking blunderbuss, strong in the thought of being master of that horrid isle, he panted for a chance to prove his potency upon the first specimen of humanity which should fall unbefriended into his hands.

Nor was he long without it. One day he spied a boat upon the beach with one man, a Negro, standing by it. Some distance off was a ship, and Oberlus immediately knew how matters stood. The vessel had put in for wood, and the boat's crew had gone into the thickets for it. From a convenient spot he kept watch of the boat, till presently a straggling company appeared loaded with billets. Throwing these on the beach, they again went into the thickets while the Negro proceeded to load the boat.

Oberlus now makes all haste and accosts the Negro, who, aghast at seeing any living being inhabiting such a solitude, and especially so horrific a one, immediately falls into a panic, not at all lessened by the ursine suavity of Oberlus who begs the favour of assisting him in his labours. The Negro stands with several billets on his shoulder, in act of shouldering others, and Oberlus, with a short cord concealed in his bosom, kindly proceeds to lift those other billets to their place. In so doing, he persists in keeping behind the Negro, who, rightly suspicious of this, in vain dodges about to gain the front of Oberlus; but Oberlus dodges also, till at last, weary of this bootless attempt at treachery, or fearful of being surprised by the remainder of the party, Oberlus runs off a little space to a bush, and, fetching his blunderbuss, savagely commands the Negro to desist work and follow him. He refuses. Whereupon presenting his piece Oberlus snaps at him. Luckily the blunderbuss misses fire, but by this time, frightened out of his wits, the Negro, upon a second intrepid summons, drops his billets, surrenders at discretion, and follows on. By a narrow defile familiar to him, Oberlus speedily removes out of sight of the water.

On their way up the mountains, he exultingly informs the Negro that henceforth he is to work for him and be his slave, and that his treatment would entirely depend on his future conduct. But Oberlus, deceived by the first impulsive cowardice of the black, in an evil moment slackens his vigilance. Passing through a narrow way, and perceiving his leader quite off his guard, the Negro, powerful fellow, suddenly grasps him in his arms, throws him down, wrests his musketoon from him, ties his hands with the monster's own cord, shoulders him, and returns with him down to the boat. When the rest of the party arrive, Oberlus is carried on board the ship. This proved an Englishman, and a smuggler, a sort of craft not apt to be over-charitable. Oberlus is severely whipped, then handcuffed, taken ashore, and compelled to make known his habitation and produce his property. His potatoes, pumpkins, and tortoises, with a pile of dollars he had hoarded from his mercantile operations, were secured on the spot. But while the too vindictive smugglers were busy destroying his hut and garden, Oberlus makes his escape into the mountains, and conceals himself there in impenetrable recesses, only known to himself, till the ship sails, when he ventures back, and by means of an old file which he sticks into a tree, contrives to free himself from his handcuffs.

Brooding among the ruins of his hut, and the desolate clinkers and extinct volcanoes of this outcast isle, the insulted misanthrope now meditates a signal revenge upon humanity, but conceals his purposes. Vessels still touch the landing at times, and by and by Oberlus is enabled to supply them with some vegetables.

Warned by his former failure in kidnapping strangers, he now pursues a quite different plan. When seamen come ashore, he makes up to them like a free and easy comrade, invites them to his hut, and with whatever affability his redhaired grimness may assume, entreats them to drink his liquor and be merry. But his guests need little pressing, and so, soon as rendered insensible, are tied hand and foot, and, pitched among the clinkers, are there concealed till the ship departs, when, finding themselves entirely dependent upon Oberlus, alarmed at his changed demeanour, his savage threats, and above all, that shocking blunderbuss, they willingly enlist under him, becoming his humble slaves, and Oberlus the most incredible of tyrants. So much so that two or three perish beneath his initiating process. He sets the remainder – four of them – to breaking the caked soil, transporting upon their backs loads of loamy earth, scooped up in moist clefts among the mountains; keeps them on the roughest fare; presents his piece at the slightest hint of insurrection; and in all respects converts them into reptiles at his feet – plebeian garter snakes to this Lord Anaconda.

At last Oberlus contrives to stock his arsenal with four rusty cutlasses and an added supply of powder and ball intended for his blunderbuss. Remitting in good part the labour of his slaves, he now approves himself a man, or rather devil, of great abilities in the way of cajoling or coercing others into acquiescence with his own ulterior designs, however at first abhorrent to them. But indeed, prepared for almost any eventual evil by their previous lawless life, as a sort of ranging cowboys of the sea, which had dissolved within them the whole moral man so that they were ready to concrete in the first offered mould of baseness now; rotted down from manhood by their hopeless misery on the isle, wonted to cringe in all things to their lord, himself the worst of slaves, these wretches were now become wholly corrupted to his hands. He used them as creatures of an inferior race; in short, he gaffles his four animals and makes murderers of them, out of cowards fitly manufacturing bravos.

Now, sword or dagger, human arms are but artificial

claws and fangs, tied on like false spurs to the fighting cock. So, we repeat, Oberlus, tsar of the isle, gaffles his four subjects; that is, with intent of glory, puts four rusty cutlasses into their hands. Like any other autocrat, he had a noble army now.

It might be thought a servile war would hereupon ensue. Arms in the hands of trodden slaves? How indiscreet of Emperor Oberlus! Nay, they had but cutlasses – sad old scythes enough – he a blunderbuss, which by its blind scatterings of all sorts of boulders, clinkers, and other scoria would annihilate all four mutineers, like four pigeons at one shot. Besides, at first he did not sleep in his accustomed hut; every lurid sunset for a time he might have been seen wending his way among the riven mountains, there to secrete himself till dawn in some sulphurous pitfall, undiscoverable to his gang. But finding this at last too troublesome, he now each evening tied his slaves hand and foot, hid the cutlasses, and thrusting them into his barracks, shut to the door, and, lying down before it, beneath a rude shed lately added, slept out the night, blunderbuss in hand.

It is supposed that not content with daily parading over a cindery solitude at the head of his fine army, Oberlus now meditated the most active mischief, his probable object being to surprise some passing ship touching at his dominions, massacre the crew, and run away with her to parts unknown. While these plans were simmering in his head, two ships touch in company at the isle, on the opposite side to his, when his designs undergo a sudden change.

The ships are in want of vegetables, which Oberlus promises in great abundance, provided they send their boats round to his landing, so that the crews may bring the vegetables from his garden, informing the two captains at the same time that his rascals – slaves and soldiers – had become so abominably lazy and good-for-nothing of late, that he could not make them work by ordinary inducements, and did not have the heart to be severe with them.

The arrangement was agreed to, and the boats were sent and hauled upon the beach. The crews went to the lava hut, but to their surprise nobody was there. After waiting till their patience was exhausted, they returned to the shore, when lo, some stranger – not the Good Samaritan either – seems to have very recently passed that way. Three of the boats were broken in a thousand pieces, and the fourth was missing. By hard toil over the mountains and through the clinkers, some of the strangers succeeded in returning to that side of the isle where the ships lay, when fresh boats are sent to the relief of the rest of the hapless party.

However amazed at the treachery of Oberlus, the two captains, afraid of new and still more mysterious atrocities – and indeed, half imputing such strange events to the enchantments associated with these isles – perceive no security but in instant flight, leaving Oberlus and his army in quiet possession of the stolen boat.

On the eve of sailing they put a letter in a keg, giving the Pacific Ocean intelligence of the affair, and moored the keg in the bay. Some time subsequent, the keg was opened by another captain chancing to anchor there, but not until after he had dispatched a boat round to Oberlus's Landing. As may be readily surmised, he felt no little inquietude till the boat's return, when another letter was handed him, giving Oberlus's version of the affair. This precious document had been found pinned half-mildewed to the clinker wall of the sulphurous and deserted hut. It ran as follows, showing that Oberlus was at least an accomplished writer, and no mere boor, and what is more, was capable of the most tristful eloquence:

Sir,

I am the most unfortunate ill-treated gentleman that lives. I am a patriot, exiled from my country by the cruel hand of tyranny.

Banished to these Enchanted Isles, I have again and again besought captains of ships to sell me a boat, but always have been refused, though I offered the handsomest prices in Mexican dollars. At length an opportunity presented of possessing myself of one, and I did not let it slip.

I have been long endeavouring, by hard labour and much solitary suffering, to accumulate something to make myself comfortable in a virtuous though unhappy old age; but at various times have been robbed and beaten by men professing to be Christians.

Today I sail from the Enchanted group in the good boat Charity bound to the Fiji Isles.

– Fatherless Oberlus.

P.S. – Behind the clinkers, nigh the oven, you will find the old fowl. Do not kill it; be patient; I leave it setting; if it shall have any chicks, I hereby bequeath them to you, whoever you may be. But don't count your chicks before they are hatched.

The fowl proved a starveling rooster, reduced to a sitting posture by sheer debility.

Oberlus declares that he was bound to the Fiji Isles; but

this was only to throw pursuers on a false scent. For, after a long time, he arrived, alone in his open boat, at Guayaquil. As his miscreants were never again beheld on Hood's Isle it is supposed either that they perished for want of water on the passage to Guayaquil or, what is quite as probable, were thrown overboard by Oberlus when he found the water growing scarce.

From Guayaquil Oberlus proceeded to Paita, and there, with that nameless witchery peculiar to some of the ugliest animals, wound himself into the affections of a tawny damsel, prevailing upon her to accompany him back to his Enchanted Isle; which doubtless he painted as a paradise of flowers, not a Tartarus of clinkers. But unfortunately for the colonisation of Hood's Isle with a choice variety of animated nature, the extraordinary and devilish aspect of Oberlus made him to be regarded in Paita as a highly suspicious character. So that being found concealed one night, with matches in his pocket, under the hull of a small vessel just ready to be launched, he was seized and thrown into jail.

The jails in most South American towns are generally of the least wholesome sort. Built of huge cakes of sunburnt brick, and containing but one room, without windows or yard, and but one door heavily grated with wooden bars, they present both within and without the grimmest aspect. As public edifices they conspicuously stand upon the hot and dusty plaza, offering to view, through the gratings, their villainous and hopeless inmates, burrowing in all sorts of tragic squalor. And here, for a long time, Oberlus was seen, the central figure of a mongrel and assassin band, a creature whom it is religion to detest, since it is philanthropy to hate a misanthrope.

Note. – They who may be disposed to question the possibility of the character above depicted are referred to the second volume of Porter's *Voyage into the Pacific*, where they will recognise many sentences, for expedition's sake derived verbatim from thence and incorporated here; the main difference – save a few passing reflections – between the two accounts being that the present writer has added to Porter's facts accessory ones picked up in the Pacific from reliable sources, and, where facts conflict, has naturally preferred his own authorities to Porter's. As, for instance, *his* authorities place Oberlus on Hood's Isle; Porter's, on Charles's Isle. The letter found in the hut is also somewhat different, for while at the Encantadas he was informed that, not only did it evince a certain clerkliness, but was full of the strangest satiric effrontery which does not adequately appear in Porter's version. I accordingly altered it to suit the general character of its author.

Sketch Tenth
Runaways, Castaways, Solitaries, Gravestones, etc.

And all about old stocks and stubs of trees,
Whereon nor fruit nor leaf was ever seen,
Did hang upon ragged knotty knees,
On which had many wretches hanged been.

Some relics of the hut of Oberlus partially remain to this day at the head of the clinkered valley. Nor does the stranger, wandering among other of the Enchanted Isles, fail to stumble upon still other solitary abodes, long abandoned to the tortoise and the lizard. Probably few parts of earth have, in modern times, sheltered so many solitaries. The reason is that these isles are situated in a distant sea, and the vessels which occasionally visit them are mostly all whalers, or ships bound on dreary and protracted voyages, exempting them in a good degree from both the oversight and the memory of human law. Such is the character of some commanders and some seamen that under these untoward circumstances it is quite impossible but that scenes of unpleasantness and discord should occur between them. A sullen hatred of the tyrannic ship will seize the sailor, and he gladly exchanges it for isles, which, though blighted as by a continual sirocco and burning breeze, still offer him, in their labyrinthine interior, a retreat beyond the possibility of capture. To flee the ship in any Peruvian or Chilean port, even the smallest and most rustical, is not unattended with great risk of apprehension, not to speak of jaguars. A reward of five pesos sends fifty dastardly Spaniards into the wood, who, with long knives, scour them day and night in eager hopes of securing their prey. Neither is it, in general, much easier to escape pursuit at the isles of Polynesia. Those of them which have felt a civilising influence present the same difficulty to the runaway with the Peruvian ports, the advanced natives being quite as mercenary and keen of knife and scent as the retrograde Spaniards; while, owing to the bad odour in which all Europeans lie, in the minds of aboriginal savages who have chanced to hear aught of them, to desert the ship among primitive Polynesians, is in most cases a hope not unforlorn. Hence the Enchanted Isles become the voluntary tarrying place of all sorts of refugees; some of whom too sadly experience the fact that flight from tyranny does not of itself ensure a safe asylum, far less a happy home.

Moreover, it has not seldom happened that hermits have been made upon the isles by the accidents incident to tortoise hunting. The interior of most of them is tangled and difficult of passage beyond description; the air is sultry and stifling; an intolerable thirst is provoked for which no running stream offers its kind relief. In a few hours, under an equatorial sun, reduced by these causes to entire exhaustion, woe betide the straggler at the Enchanted Isles! Their extent is such as to forbid an adequate search, unless weeks are devoted to it. The impatient ship waits a day or two, when, the missing man remaining undiscovered, up goes a stake on the beach, with a letter of regret, and a keg of crackers and another of water tied to it, and away sails the craft.

Nor have there been wanting instances where the inhumanity of some captains has led them to wreak a secure revenge upon seamen who have given their caprice or pride some singular offence. Thrust ashore upon the scorching marl, such mariners are abandoned to perish outright, unless by solitary labours they succeed in discovering some precious dribblets of moisture oozing from a rock or stagnant in a mountain pool.

I was well acquainted with a man who, lost upon the Isle of Narborough, was brought to such extremes by thirst that at last he only saved his life by taking that of another being.

A large hair seal came upon the beach. He rushed upon it, stabbed it in the neck, and then throwing himself upon the panting body quaffed at the living wound; the palpitations of the creature's dying heart injected life into the drinker.

Another seaman, thrust ashore in a boat upon an isle at which no ship ever touched owing to its peculiar sterility and the shoals about it, and from which all other parts of the group were hidden – this man, feeling that it was sure death to remain there, and that nothing worse than death menaced him in quitting it, killed two seals, and, inflating their skins, made a float, upon which he transported himself to Charles's Island, and joined the republic there.

But men not endowed with courage equal to such desperate attempts find their only resource in forthwith seeking some watering place, however precarious or scanty, building a hut, catching tortoises and birds, and in all respects preparing for a hermit life, till tide or time, or a passing ship, arrives to float them off.

At the foot of precipices on many of the isles, small rude basins in the rocks are found, partly filled with rotted rubbish or vegetable decay, or overgrown with thickets, and sometimes a little moist, which, upon examination, reveal plain tokens of artificial instruments employed in hollowing them out, by some poor castaway or still more miserable runaway. These basins are made in places where it was supposed some scanty drops of dew might exude into them from the upper crevices.

The relics of hermitages and stone basins are not the only signs of vanishing humanity to be found upon the isles. And, curious to say, that spot which of all others in settled communities is most animated, at the Enchanted Isles presents the most dreary of aspects. And though it may seem very strange to talk of post offices in this barren region, yet post offices are occasionally to be found there. They consist of a stake and a bottle. The letters being not only sealed, but corked. They are generally deposited by captains of Nantucketers for the benefit of passing fishermen, and contain statements as to what luck they had in whaling or tortoise hunting. Frequently, however, long months and months, whole years glide by and no applicant appears. The stake rots and falls, presenting no very exhilarating object.

If now it be added that gravestones, or rather graveboards, are also discovered upon some of the isles, the picture will be complete.

Upon the beach of James's Isle, for many years was to be seen a rude fingerpost, pointing inland. And, perhaps, taking it for some signal of possible hospitality in this otherwise desolate spot – some good hermit living there with his maple dish – the stranger would follow on in the path thus indicated, till at last he would come out in a noiseless nook and find his only welcome, a dead man – his sole greeting the inscription over a grave. Here in 1813 fell, in a daybreak duel, a lieutenant of the US frigate *Essex*, aged twenty-one – attaining his majority in death.

It is but fit that, like those old monastic institutions of Europe whose inmates go not out of their own walls to be inurned but are entombed there where they die, the Encantadas, too, should bury their own dead, even as the great general monastery of earth does hers.

It is known that burial in the ocean is a pure necessity of seafaring life, and that it is only done when land is far astern, and not clearly visible from the bow. Hence, to vessels cruising in the vicinity of the Enchanted Isles, they afford a convenient Potter's Field. The interment over, some good-natured forecastle poet and artist seizes his paint brush and inscribes a doggerel epitaph. When, after a long lapse of time, other good-natured seamen chance to come upon the spot, they usually make a table of the mound, and quaff a friendly can to the poor soul's repose.

As a specimen of these epitaphs, take the following, found in a bleak gorge of Chatham Isle:

Oh, Brother Jack, as you pass by,
As you are now, so once was I.
Just so game, and just so gay,
But now, alack, they've stopped my pay.
No more I peep out of my blinkers,
Here I be – tucked in with clinkers!

NOTES

1. Idumea (Edom) was an ancient kingdom situated between Palestine and Egypt.

2. Albemarle Island (Isla Isabela) is the largest of the islands in the Galapagos.

3. Pisgah is a mountain range east of the River Jordan, where Moses caught sight of the promised land.

4. Daniel Boone (1734–1820) was an American pioneer and a key figure in the settlement of Kentucky.

5. Narborough, also called Fernandina, is located to the west of Albemarle.

6. English buccaneer Ambrose Cowley was an early explorer of the Galapagos, and responsible for the first navigation charts of the islands in 1684.

7. William Dampier (1652–1715) was a British explorer and one of the foremost navigators of his day; Lionel Wafer (1640–1705) was a Welsh surgeon who made a number of voyages on board merchant ships, often accompanying William Dampier.

8. The character of Oberlus is based on Irish-born Patrick Watkins who was marooned on the Galapagos Islands in 1807 where he remained for two years.

BIOGRAPHICAL NOTE

Herman Melville was born in New York in 1819 into an established family of merchants. However, the family's fortunes soon changed. Their business failed and Melville's father died in 1832. As a result Melville left school and was forced to teach himself. An avid reader, he devoured the works of Shakespeare, the Bible, and many seventeenth-century historical and anthropological writings.

Giving up his work as a farm labourer, Melville sailed to Liverpool in 1839. From there he sailed to the South Seas on board the whaler *Acushnet*, whereupon he jumped ship and enrolled in the US Navy. Some three years later, having lived briefly with the Typee cannibals in the Marquesas Islands, he returned home to begin writing.

Typee, a fictionalised account of his time with the cannibals, was published first in Britain in 1846. This remained his most popular work during his lifetime. Its sequel, *Omoo*, followed in 1847. After a number of other works, which had a mixed reception, he went on, perhaps inspired by the success of Hawthorne, to write *Moby-Dick* (1851). In subsequent years, and after various further publications, his popularity waned, and by the time of his death in 1891, he was largely forgotten.

HESPERUS PRESS – 100 PAGES

Hesperus Press, as suggested by the Latin motto, is committed to bringing near what is far – far both in space and time. Works written by the greatest authors, and unjustly neglected or simply little known in the English-speaking world, are made accessible through new translations and a completely fresh editorial approach. Through these short classic works, each little more than 100 pages in length, the reader will be introduced to the greatest writers from all times and all cultures.

For more information on Hesperus Press, please visit our website: **www.hesperuspress.com**

To place an order, please contact:
Grantham Book Services
Isaac Newton Way
Alma Park Industrial Estate
Grantham
Lincolnshire NG31 9SD
Tel: +44 (0) 1476 541080
Fax: +44 (0) 1476 541061
Email: orders@gbs.tbs-ltd.co.uk

SELECTED TITLES FROM HESPERUS PRESS